PERSPECTIVE

Insights from 1 and 2 Thessalonians

MELANIE NEWTON

JOYFUL
WALK
BIBLE
STUDIES

We extend our heartfelt thanks to the many women who served as contributors to the original study guide, especially Joan Floyd and Robin Colley. We also are so appreciative to all those who served as editors for the lessons in this revised study—Nancy Stephenson, Julia Gendron, Aimee Jones, Marlyn Scott, Connie Crowley, Heather Newton, Vanessa Morris, Kim Newton, Lida Lowey, and Sandy Sims. Your work is much appreciated.

Perspective: Insights from 1 and 2 Thessalonians

© 2025 Melanie Newton. All rights reserved.

Published by Joyful Walk Press, Flower Mound, TX

ISBN: 979-8-9925303-1-5

For questions about the use of this study guide or for bulk orders, please email us at melanienewton.com/contact.

Cover graphic is a public domain image provided by Charl van Rooy on unsplash.com. The map on page 11 is adapted from the public domain image, "second_missionary_journey-1024x604.jpg."

Melanie Newton is the author of "Graceful Beginnings" books for anyone new to the Bible and "Joyful Walk Bible Studies" for established Christians. Her mission is to help women learn to study the Bible for themselves and to grow their Bible-teaching skills to lead others.

Joyful Walk Bible Studies are grace-based studies for women of all ages. Each study guide follows the inductive method of Bible study (observation, interpretation, application) in a warm and inviting format. We pray that you and your group will find *Perspective* a resource that God will use to strengthen you in your faith walk with Him.

Christ-Focused • Grace-Based • Bible-Rich

JOYFUL WALK PRESS
Flower Mound, TX

MELANIE NEWTON

Melanie Newton is a Louisiana girl who made the choice to follow Jesus while attending LSU. She and her husband Ron married and moved to Texas for him to attend Dallas Theological Seminary. They stayed in Texas where Ron led a wilderness camping ministry for troubled youth for many years. Ron now helps corporations with their challenging employees and is the author of the top-rated business book, *No Jerks on the Job*.

Melanie jumped into raising three Texas-born children and serving in ministry to women at her church. Through the years, the Lord has given her opportunity to do Bible teaching and to write grace-based Bible studies for women that are now available from her website (melanienewton.com) and on Bible.org. *Graceful Beginnings* books are for anyone new to the Bible. *Joyful Walk Bible Studies* are for maturing Christians.

Melanie Newton loves to help women learn how to study the Bible for themselves. She also teaches online courses for women to grow their Bible-teaching skills to help others—all with the goal of getting to know Jesus more along the way. Her heart's desire is to encourage you to have a joyful relationship with Jesus Christ so you are willing to share that experience with others around you.

Jesus took hold of me in 1972, and I've been on this great adventure ever since. My life is a gift of God, full of blessings in the midst of difficult challenges. The more I've learned and experienced God's absolutely amazing grace, the more I've discovered my faith walk to be a joyful one. I'm still seeking that joyful walk every day.

Melanie

OTHER BIBLE STUDIES BY MELANIE NEWTON

Graceful Beginnings Series books for anyone new to the Bible:

A Fresh Start (basics for new Christians)
Painting the Portrait of Jesus (the Gospel of John)
The God You Can Know (the character of God)
Grace Overflowing (an overview of Paul's 13 letters)
The Walk from Fear to Faith (Old Testament women)
Satisfied by His Love (women who knew Jesus)
Seek the Treasure (study of Ephesians)
Pathways to a Joyful Walk (6 pathways to a life filled with joy)

Joyful Walk Bible Studies for growing Christians:

Adorn Yourself with Godliness (1 Timothy and Titus, also in Spanish)
Everyday Women, Ever Faithful God (Old Testament women, also in Spanish)
Connecting Faith to Life on Planet Earth (Genesis 1-11; Revelation)
Graceful Living (the essentials for a grace-based Christian life)
Graceful Living Today (a devotional journal for a joyful life)
Healthy Living (Colossians and Philemon)
Heartbreak to Hope (the Gospel of Mark)
Identity: Sticking to Your Faith in a Pull-Apart World (Ezra thru Malachi)
Knowing Jesus, Knowing Joy (Philippians, also in Spanish)
Live Out His Love (New Testament women)
Perspective (1and 2 Thessalonians)
Profiles of Perseverance (Old Testament men, also in Spanish)
Radical Acts (Acts)
Reboot, Renew, Rejoice (1 and 2 Chronicles)
The God-Dependent Woman (2 Corinthians)
To Be Found Faithful (2 Timothy)

Resources for leading others

Be a Christ-Focused Small Group Leader
Leap into Lifestyle Disciplemaking
Bible Study Leadership Made Easy (online video course)
Painting the Picture of Jesus (the "I Am's" of Jesus lessons for children)
Teaching Children the God They Can Know (the character of God for children)

Download our catalogue and get resources for your spiritual growth at melanienewton.com.

Contents

Using This Study Guide

This study guide consists of 11 lessons covering two of Paul's letters—1 and 2 Thessalonians. The lessons are divided into 4 sections (about 20 minutes in length). The first 3 sections contain a detail study of the passages. The last section is a podcast that provides additional insight to the lesson.

If you cannot do the entire lesson one week, please read the "Day One Study" and listen to the podcast.

The extra lesson at the end covers Bible passages referring to the future Millennial Kingdom and life after that time on the new earth.

THE BASIC STUDY

Each lesson includes core questions covering the passage narrative. These core questions will take you through the process of inductive Bible study—observation, interpretation, and application. It is the best approach for doing Bible Study. The process is more easily understood in the context of answering these questions:

- What does the passage say? (**Observation**: what is actually there)
- What does it mean? (**Interpretation**: the author's intended meaning)
- How does this apply to me today? (**Application**: making it personal) Some questions introduced with the words "Gain perspective" also fit the application category.

STUDY ENHANCEMENTS

Deeper Discoveries: Embedded within the sections are *optional* questions for research of subjects we do not have time to cover adequately in the lessons or contain information that significantly enhance the basic study. If you are meeting with a small group, your leader may give you the opportunity to share your "discoveries."

Study Aids: To aid in proper interpretation and application of the study, additional study aids are located where appropriate in the lesson:

- Historical Insight
- Scriptural Insight
- From the Greek (definitions of Greek words)
- Focus on the Meaning
- Think About It (thoughtful reflection)
- Dependent Living (relying on Christ)

Other useful study tools: Use online tools or apps (blueletterbible.org or "Blue Letter Bible app" is especially helpful) to find *cross references* (verses with similar content to what you are studying) and meanings of the *original Greek words or phrases* used (usually called "interlinear"). You can also look at any verse in *various Bible translations* to help with understanding what it is saying.

PODCASTS

Find podcasts for these lessons at melanienewton.com/podcasts (choose "13: Thessalonians) and on most podcast providers. Or you can read the blogs associated with the podcasts at melanienewton.com/blog. Choose 1 & 2 Thessalonians category then scroll to find the title you want. Listen to the first podcast as an introduction to the study.

NEW TESTAMENT SUMMARY

The New Testament opens with the births of John and Jesus. About 30 years later, John challenged the Jews to indicate their repentance (turning from sin and toward God) by submitting to water baptism—a familiar Old Testament practice used for repentance as well as when a Gentile converted to Judaism (to be washed clean of idolatry).

Jesus, God's incarnate Son, publicly showed the world what God is like and taught His perfect ways for 3 – 3½ years. After preparing 12 disciples to continue Christ's earthly work, He died voluntarily on a cross for mankind's sin, rose from the dead, and returned to heaven. The account of His earthly life is recorded in 4 books known as the Gospels (the biblical books of Matthew, Mark, Luke and John named after the compiler of each account).

After Jesus' return to heaven, the followers of Christ were then empowered by the Holy Spirit and spread God's salvation message among the Jews, a number of whom believed in Christ. The apostle Paul and others carried the good news to the Gentiles during 3 missionary journeys (much of this recorded in the book of Acts). Paul wrote 13 New Testament letters to churches & individuals (Romans through Philemon). The section in our Bible from Hebrews to Jude contains 8 additional letters penned by five men, including two apostles (Peter and John) and two of Jesus' half-brothers (James and Jude). The author of Hebrews is unknown. The apostle John also recorded Revelation, which summarizes God's final program for the world. The Bible ends as it began—with a new, sinless creation.

DISCUSSION GROUP GUIDELINES

1. **Attend consistently** whether your lesson is done or not. You will learn from the other women, and they want to get to know you.

2. **Set aside time** to work through the study questions. The goal of Bible study is to **get to know** Jesus. He will change your life.

3. **Share your insights** from your personal study time. As you spend time in the Bible, Jesus will teach you truth through His Spirit inside you.

4. **Respect each other's insights**. Listen thoughtfully. Encourage each other as you interact. Refrain from dominating the discussion if you have a tendency to be talkative. ☺

5. **Celebrate our unity** in Christ. Avoid bringing up controversial subjects such as politics, divisive issues, and denominational differences.

6. **Maintain confidentiality.** Remember that anything shared during the group time is not to leave the **group** (unless permission is granted by the one sharing).

7. **Pray for one another** as sisters in Christ.

8. **Get to know the women** in your group. Please do not use your small group members for solicitation purposes for home businesses, though.

There is a small group discussion guide available at the end of this study. Anyone can use the guide to lead a group through a discussion of the questions in this study. This is especially useful for groups that have less than two hours to meet together.

Enjoy your Joyful Walk Bible Study!

Paul's First Letter to the Thessalonians (NIV 2011)

Paul, Silas and Timothy,

To the church of the Thessalonians in God the Father and the Lord Jesus Christ:

Grace and peace to you.

We always thank God for all of you and continually mention you in our prayers. We remember before our God and Father your work produced by faith, your labor prompted by love, and your endurance inspired by hope in our Lord Jesus Christ.

For we know, brothers and sisters loved by God, that he has chosen you, because our gospel came to you not simply with words but also with power, with the Holy Spirit and deep conviction. You know how we lived among you for your sake. You became imitators of us and of the Lord, for you welcomed the message in the midst of severe suffering with the joy given by the Holy Spirit. And so, you became a model to all the believers in Macedonia and Achaia. The Lord's message rang out from you not only in Macedonia and Achaia—your faith in God has become known everywhere. Therefore, we do not need to say anything about it, for they themselves report what kind of reception you gave us. They tell how you turned to God from idols to serve the living and true God, and to wait for his Son from heaven, whom he raised from the dead—Jesus, who rescues us from the coming wrath.

You know, brothers and sisters, that our visit to you was not without results. We had previously suffered and been treated outrageously in Philippi, as you know, but with the help of our God we dared to tell you his gospel in the face of strong opposition. For the appeal we make does not spring from error or impure motives, nor are we trying to trick you. On the contrary, we speak as those approved by God to be entrusted with the gospel. We are not trying to please people but God, who tests our hearts. You know we never used flattery, nor did we put on a mask to cover up greed—God is our witness. We were not looking for praise from people, not from you or anyone else, even though as apostles of Christ we could have asserted our authority. Instead, we were like young children among you.

Just as a nursing mother cares for her children, so we cared for you. Because we loved you so much, we were delighted to share with you not only the gospel of God but our lives as well. Surely you remember, brothers and sisters, our toil and hardship; we worked night and day in order not to be a burden to anyone while we preached the gospel of God to you. You are witnesses, and so is God, of how holy, righteous and blameless we were among you who believed. For you know that we dealt with each of you as a father deals with his own children, encouraging, comforting and urging you to live lives worthy of God, who calls you into his kingdom and glory.

And we also thank God continually because, when you received the word of God, which you heard from us, you accepted it not as a human word, but as it actually is, the word of God, which is indeed at work in you who believe. For you, brothers and sisters, became imitators of God's churches in Judea, which are in Christ Jesus: You suffered from your own people the same things those churches suffered from the Jews who killed the Lord Jesus and the prophets and also drove us out. They displease God and are hostile to everyone in their effort to keep us from speaking to the Gentiles so that they may be saved. In this way, they always heap up their sins to the limit. The wrath of God has come upon them at last.

But, brothers and sisters, when we were orphaned by being separated from you for a short time (in person, not in thought), out of our intense longing we made every effort to see you. For we wanted to come to you—certainly I, Paul, did, again and again—but Satan blocked our way. For what is our hope, our joy, or the crown in which we will glory in the presence of our Lord Jesus when he comes? Is it not you? Indeed, you are our glory and joy.

So, when we could stand it no longer, we thought it best to be left by ourselves in Athens. We sent Timothy, who is our brother and co-worker in God's service in spreading the gospel of Christ, to strengthen and encourage you in your faith, so that no one would be unsettled by these trials. For you know quite well that we are destined for them. In fact, when we were with you, we kept telling you that we would be persecuted. And it turned out that way, as you well know. For this reason, when I could stand it no longer, I sent to find out about your faith. I was afraid that in some way the tempter had tempted you and that our labors might have been in vain.

But Timothy has just now come to us from you and has brought good news about your faith and love. He has told us that you always have pleasant memories of us and that you long to see us, just as we also long to see you. Therefore, brothers and sisters, in all our distress and persecution we were encouraged about you because of your faith. For now we really live, since you are standing firm in the Lord. How can we thank God enough for you in return for all the joy we have in the presence of our God because of you? Night and day we pray most earnestly that we may see you again and supply what is lacking in your faith.

Now may our God and Father Himself and our Lord Jesus clear the way for us to come to you. May the Lord make your love increase and overflow for each other and for everyone else, just as ours does for you. May He strengthen your hearts so that you will be blameless and holy in the presence of our God and Father when our Lord Jesus comes with all His holy ones.

As for other matters, brothers and sisters, we instructed you how to live in order to please God, as in fact you are living. Now we ask you and urge you in the Lord Jesus to do this more and more. For you know what instructions we gave you by the authority of the Lord Jesus.

It is God's will that you should be sanctified: that you should avoid sexual immorality; that each of you should learn to control your own body in a way that is holy and honorable, not in passionate lust like the pagans, who do not know God; and that in this matter no one should wrong or take advantage of a brother or sister. The Lord will punish all those who commit such sins, as we told you and warned you before. For God did not call us to be impure, but to live a holy life. Therefore, anyone who rejects this instruction does not reject a human being but God, the very God who gives you his Holy Spirit.

Now about your love for one another we do not need to write to you, for you yourselves have been taught by God to love each other. And in fact, you do love all of God's family throughout Macedonia. Yet we urge you, brothers and sisters, to do so more and more, and to make it your ambition to lead a quiet life: You should mind your own business and work with your hands, just as we told you, so that your daily life may win the respect of outsiders and so that you will not be dependent on anybody.

Brothers and sisters, we do not want you to be uninformed about those who sleep in death, so that you do not grieve like the rest of mankind, who have no hope. For we believe that Jesus died and rose again, and so we believe that God will bring with Jesus those who have fallen asleep in him. According to the Lord's word, we tell you that we who are still alive, who are left until the coming of the Lord, will certainly not precede those who have fallen asleep. For the Lord himself will come down from heaven, with a loud command, with the voice of the archangel and with the trumpet call of God, and the dead in Christ will rise first. After that, we who are still alive and are left will be caught up together with them in the clouds to meet the Lord in the air. And so we will be with the Lord forever. Therefore, encourage one another with these words.

Now, brothers and sisters, about times and dates we do not need to write to you, for you know very well that the day of the Lord will come like a thief in the night. While people are saying, "Peace and safety," destruction will come on them suddenly, as labor pains on a pregnant woman, and they will not escape.

But you, brothers and sisters, are not in darkness so that this day should surprise you like a thief. You are all children of the light and children of the day. We do not belong to the night or to the darkness. So then, let us not be like others, who are asleep, but let us be awake and sober. For those who sleep, sleep at night, and those who get drunk, get drunk at night. But since we belong to the day, let us be sober, putting on faith and love as a breastplate, and the hope of salvation as a helmet. For God did not appoint us to suffer wrath but to receive salvation through our Lord Jesus Christ. He died for us so that, whether we are awake or asleep, we may live together with him. Therefore, encourage one another and build each other up, just as in fact you are doing.

Now we ask you, brothers and sisters, to acknowledge those who work hard among you, who care for you in the Lord and who admonish you. Hold them in the highest regard in love because of their work. Live in peace with each other. And we urge you, brothers and sisters, warn those who are idle and disruptive, encourage the disheartened, help the weak, be patient with everyone. Make sure that nobody pays back wrong for wrong, but always strive to do what is good for each other and for everyone else.

Rejoice always, pray continually, give thanks in all circumstances; for this is God's will for you in Christ Jesus.

Do not quench the Spirit. Do not treat prophecies with contempt but test them all; hold on to what is good, reject every kind of evil.

May God himself, the God of peace, sanctify you through and through. May your whole spirit, soul and body be kept blameless at the coming of our Lord Jesus Christ. The one who calls you is faithful, and he will do it.

Brothers and sisters, pray for us. Greet all God's people with a holy kiss. I charge you before the Lord to have this letter read to all the brothers and sisters.

The grace of our Lord Jesus Christ be with you.

Paul's Second Letter to the Thessalonians (NIV 2011)

Paul, Silas and Timothy,

To the church of the Thessalonians in God our Father and the Lord Jesus Christ:

Grace and peace to you from God the Father and the Lord Jesus Christ.

We ought always to thank God for you, brothers and sisters, and rightly so, because your faith is growing more and more, and the love all of you have for one another is increasing. Therefore, among God's churches we boast about your perseverance and faith in all the persecutions and trials you are enduring.

All this is evidence that God's judgment is right, and as a result you will be counted worthy of the kingdom of God, for which you are suffering. God is just: He will pay back trouble to those who trouble you and give relief to you who are troubled, and to us as well. This will happen when the Lord Jesus is revealed from heaven in blazing fire with his powerful angels. He will punish those who do not know God and do not obey the gospel of our Lord Jesus. They will be punished with everlasting destruction and shut out from the presence of the Lord and from the glory of his might on the day he comes to be glorified in his holy people and to be marveled at among all those who have believed. This includes you, because you believed our testimony to you.

With this in mind, we constantly pray for you, that our God may make you worthy of his calling, and that by his power he may bring to fruition your every desire for goodness and your every deed prompted by faith. We pray this so that the name of our Lord Jesus may be glorified in you, and you in him, according to the grace of our God and the Lord Jesus Christ.

Concerning the coming of our Lord Jesus Christ and our being gathered to him, we ask you, brothers and sisters, not to become easily unsettled or alarmed by the teaching allegedly from us—whether by a prophecy or by word of mouth or by letter—asserting that the day of the Lord has already come. Don't let anyone deceive you in any way, for that day will not come until the rebellion occurs and the man of lawlessness is revealed, the man doomed to destruction. He will oppose and will exalt himself over everything that is called God or is worshiped, so that he sets himself up in God's temple, proclaiming himself to be God.

Don't you remember that when I was with you I used to tell you these things? And now you know what is holding him back, so that he may be revealed at the proper time. For the secret power of lawlessness is already at work; but the one who now holds it back will continue to do so till he is taken out of the way. And then the lawless one will be revealed, whom the Lord Jesus will overthrow with the breath of his mouth and destroy by the splendor of his coming. The coming of the lawless one will be in accordance with how Satan works. He will use all sorts of displays of power through signs and wonders that serve the lie, and all the ways that wickedness deceives those who are perishing. They perish because they refused to love the truth and so be saved. For this reason, God sends them a powerful delusion so that they will believe the lie and so that all will be condemned who have not believed the truth but have delighted in wickedness.

But we ought always to thank God for you, brothers and sisters loved by the Lord, because God chose you as firstfruits to be saved through the sanctifying work of the Spirit and through belief in the truth. He called you to this through our gospel, that you might share in the glory of our Lord Jesus Christ.

So then, brothers and sisters, stand firm and hold fast to the teachings we passed on to you, whether by word of mouth or by letter.

May our Lord Jesus Christ himself and God our Father, who loved us and by his grace gave us eternal encouragement and good hope, encourage your hearts and strengthen you in every good deed and word.

As for other matters, brothers and sisters, pray for us that the message of the Lord may spread rapidly and be honored, just as it was with you. And pray that we may be delivered from wicked and evil people, for not everyone has faith. But the Lord is faithful, and he will strengthen you and protect you from the evil one. We have confidence in the Lord that you are doing and will continue to do the things we command. May the Lord direct your hearts into God's love and Christ's perseverance.

In the name of the Lord Jesus Christ, we command you, brothers and sisters, to keep away from every believer who is idle and disruptive and does not live according to the teaching you received from us. For you yourselves know how you ought to follow our example. We were not idle when we were with you, nor did we eat anyone's food without paying for it. On the contrary, we worked night and day, laboring and toiling so that we would not be a burden to any of you. We did this, not because we do not have the right to such help, but in order to offer ourselves as a model for you to imitate. For even when we were with you, we gave you this rule: "The one who is unwilling to work shall not eat."

We hear that some among you are idle and disruptive. They are not busy; they are busybodies. Such people we command and urge in the Lord Jesus Christ to settle down and earn the food they eat. And as for you, brothers and sisters, never tire of doing what is good.

Take special note of anyone who does not obey our instruction in this letter. Do not associate with them, in order that they may feel ashamed. Yet do not regard them as an enemy, but warn them as you would a fellow believer.

Now may the Lord of peace himself give you peace at all times and in every way. The Lord be with all of you.

I, Paul, write this greeting in my own hand, which is the distinguishing mark in all my letters. This is how I write.

The grace of our Lord Jesus Christ be with you all.

> *Recommended: As an introduction to the whole study, listen to the podcast "The Need for Perspective" at melanienewton.com/podcasts.*

The Need for Perspective

THE STORY

- When the apostle Paul wrote the letters that we know as 1 and 2 Thessalonians, he had been a Christian for more than 15 years. From the beginning, Jesus told Paul that he was to go to those who were called Gentiles (non-Jews) and preach the gospel to them.

- On his second missionary journey, God directed their movements first to northern Greece to the cities of Philippi and Thessalonica. Then, they went to southern Greece to the cities of Athens and Corinth. It is from Corinth that Paul wrote two letters back to the Thessalonians.

GAIN PERSPECTIVE

> Perspective is an objective assessment of any situation,
> giving all aspects their comparative importance.

- We all need perspective to help us successfully navigate through the challenges of daily life.

- Gaining perspective is like sharpening your focus with a lens. Sharpening your focus not only clears up blurry vision, but it can also help you to see something at a distance that you were not able to see. You get a glimpse of where you are heading. Paul's letters to the Thessalonian Christians helped them gain perspective about many issues of life.

- From the moment Paul entered their city, the Thessalonians knew him as being well-educated and a tent-making craftsman. They knew that he was determined, bold, convinced of the truth of Christ, and very committed to Jesus' calling on his life. He was a gifted teacher and loved God's people almost as much as he loved God Himself. Paul reminded them of that in 1 Thessalonians to help sharpen their focus on who he was and what kind of relationship he had with them. They could trust his words.

- There were no cell phones or email for Paul. He depended upon letters and eyewitness accounts for his information about all the churches. You'll see evidence of this in the Thessalonian letters.

- Biblical perspective on life is God's perspective on life. Paul helped the Thessalonians gain God's perspective on the persecution they were suffering at the hands of their neighbors. When you sharpen your focus to gain perspective, you get…

...the ability to see God's presence, to perceive God's power, and to focus on God's plan in spite of the obstacles. (Chuck Swindoll, *Insight for Today devotional,* May 19, 2017)

- Biblical perspective on life helps you grow in confidence because you learn that your self-worth is not derived from any human being but from God.

- Biblical perspective about death and the future gives you hope and assurance of your future with Christ in eternity. You will not fear death as those who have no hope.

- Knowing the future hope gives you God's perspective on life that you need in your world today. For now, you must live and work in this world. Paul's letters to the Thessalonians have a lot to say about that.

- When you gain the biblical perspective on who God is, what it means to live your life to please Him, and what He has planned for your future, you get a security in Him that allows you to rest and enjoy life today. And you will be able to serve God with greater enthusiasm and freedom to impact your world for Him.

Let Jesus satisfy your heart with His perspective on life in the present and in the future. Then, live securely in Him during this time of waiting.

1: Overview of 1 and 2 Thessalonians

DAY ONE STUDY

Ask the Lord Jesus to teach you through His Word.

The ABCs of 1 and 2 Thessalonians—Author, Background, and Context

Like any book you read, it always helps to know a bit about the author, the background setting for the story (i.e., past, present, future), and where the book fits into a series (that's the context). The same is true of Bible books.

AUTHOR

Paul identifies himself as the author of this letter written to the church of the Thessalonians. Paul, whose Hebrew name was Saul, was born in Tarsus, a major Roman city on the coast of southeast Asia Minor. Tarsus was the center for the tent-making industry. Paul was trained in that craft as his occupation (his primary paying profession). As a Jewish Pharisee from the tribe of Benjamin, Paul was educated at the feet of Gamaliel, a well-respected rabbi of the day. Paul was an ardent persecutor of the early church until his life-changing encounter with Jesus Christ.

After believing in Jesus Christ as his Savior, Paul was called by Christ to take the gospel to the Gentiles. This was an amazing about-face for a committed Pharisee like Paul who ordinarily would have nothing to do with Gentiles. He founded numerous churches and wrote 13 letters that are included in the New Testament. Tradition has it that Paul was beheaded shortly after he wrote 2 Timothy in 67 AD. *(Adapted from Acts 8:3; 9:1-31; 22:3-5; 26:9-11; and Galatians 1:11-24.)*

BACKGROUND

Located in northern Greece, Thessalonica was founded in 315 BC. Over time, it became an important urban center because of its strategic location near the Aegean Sea. In the Roman Empire, it was the capital of the province of Macedonia and its largest city with 200,000 people. Thessalonica stood on the *Via Egnatia*, the Roman version of an interstate highway, making it an important city of commerce. In Paul's day, it was a self-governing community with enough Jews in residence to warrant a synagogue (Acts 17:1).

While Paul was in Troas on his second missionary journey, God showed him a vision of a man from Macedonia saying, "Come over and help us." Paul and Silas went, stopping first at Philippi, where

they preached the gospel, and a church was formed. After spending a night in prison for driving an evil spirit from a girl, Paul and Silas were forced to leave Philippi. They went about 100 miles west to Thessalonica.

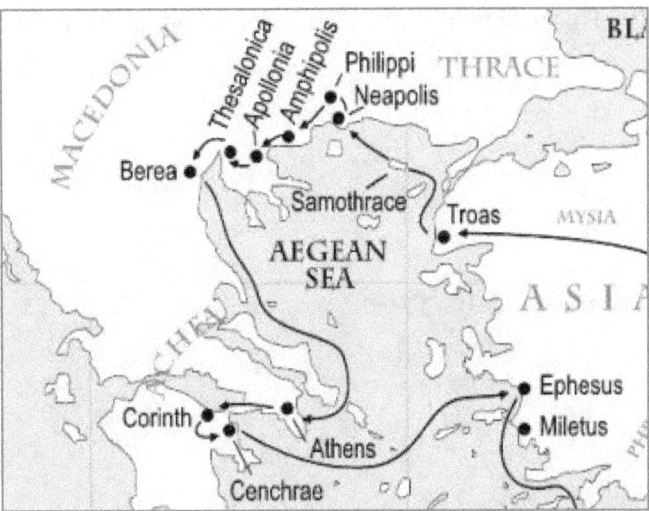

For at least three Sabbath days, Paul reasoned in the synagogue with those present, and many believed the gospel. Because of all that he accomplished in Thessalonica, he probably ministered for a longer time than just three weeks. Several Jews and many God-fearing Greeks believed, including some leading women of the city. This angered a group of unbelieving Jews who then stirred up trouble for Paul. So the Thessalonian Christians sent Paul, Silas, and Timothy away from the city by night to Berea, 50 miles to the west.

Paul and his party began their evangelistic work in Berea in the synagogue, as was their custom, and many people there believed. Sadly, the Thessalonian Jews traveled to Berea and stirred up more trouble for Paul. So the Berean Christians sent Paul away to Athens (southern Greece). But Silas and Timothy remained in Berea. While in Athens, Paul wrote to Silas and Timothy, asking them to join him there. But he soon sent Silas back to Philippi and Timothy back to Thessalonica to continue discipling those churches. Then, Paul moved to Corinth. Silas and Timothy rejoined him there, bringing a financial gift from the Christians in those Macedonian (northern Greece) towns. Timothy's report of conditions in the Thessalonian church led Paul to write the first letter from Corinth about 51 AD. Then, he wrote the second letter within 6-12 months after the first letter.

Here is a possible timeline (a best guess based on available information):

Church founded *Acts 17:1-15* **Fall/Winter 50-51**	Paul sent Timothy to Thessalonica *1 Thessalonians 3:2* **Spring 51**	Paul in Corinth *Acts 18:1-5* **Summer 51**	Timothy came with news from Thessalonica ***1 Thessalonians written and sent*** **Fall 51**	News received ***2 Thessalonians written and sent*** **Winter/Spring 52**

CONTEXT

Even though you will find 1 and 2 Thessalonians after the book of Colossians in the New Testament, the Thessalonian letters were written much earlier. In fact, they are considered to be some of the earliest of Paul's writings. Only Galatians was likely written before them. Because of the short time between the writing of the 2 letters to the Thessalonians, it makes sense to study them together as we'll be doing.

1. What grabbed your attention as you read the ABC's of the books of 1 and 2 Thessalonians?

2. Read Acts 17:1-15. What do you learn from these verses about Paul's experience in Thessalonica?

    *   Vv. 1-4—

    *   Vv. 5-10, 13—

- What events and people would still be fresh in his mind just a few months later when he wrote the letters?

Scriptural Insight: Paul's reasoning "persuaded some" in the synagogue services. His converts seem to have been mainly Gentiles, many of whom were God-fearers, or "God-fearing Greeks," but some of them were Jews. "Jason" (v. 5), Aristarchus, and Secundus appear to have been among these new believers. The "leading women" could have belonged to the upper classes, or they may have been the wives of the city's leading men. In either case, the gospel had an impact on the leadership level of society in Thessalonica. ... Three converts from Thessalonica—Sopater, Aristarchus (Acts 20:4; 27:2; Col. 4:10), and Secundus (Acts 20:4)—later traveled with Paul (Acts 20:4). Aristarchus stayed with Paul during his Caesarean imprisonment and traveled with him all the way to Rome. (*Dr. Constable's Notes on Acts 2020 Edition,* adapted from pp. 347, 350, 481)

Gain Perspective

You have probably heard the phrase, "You need to gain perspective." But what is perspective? According to the dictionary:

Perspective is an objective assessment of any situation, giving all aspects their comparative importance.

Objective assessment. Looking at all the issues and facts. That sounds like a necessary action to take whenever you must make a decision, doesn't it? We all need perspective to help us successfully navigate through the challenges of daily life.

Gaining perspective is like sharpening your focus with a lens. When you have trouble seeing, and you go to an optometrist to get your eyes checked, you come away with a prescription for glasses or contacts that will enable your eyes to focus again. When you put on those new lenses, what was once a blur has now become clear. That's what happens when you gain perspective.

Sharpening your focus not only clears up blurry vision, but it can also help us to see something at a distance that we were not able to see. Consider how a pair of binoculars works. Let's say you are driving down a highway to get to the mountains. You go around a curve, and there they are in the distance. You get excited about your journey there. But you need help to see them. So you pull out a pair of binoculars and focus on the mountain peaks in the distance. You get a glimpse of where you are heading.

That's what Paul's letters to the Thessalonian Christians helped them to do. They gained perspective about a bunch of things.

Biblical perspective on life is God's perspective on life. Paul helped the Thessalonians gain God's perspective on the persecution they were suffering at the hands of their neighbors. Having the biblical perspective about suffering helps you to stand firm and press onward regardless of obstacles in your life.

Biblical perspective on life helps you grow in confidence because you learn that your self-worth is not derived from any human being but from God. This gives you stability, certainty, and confidence in your God who is faithful to you. Others will notice and be benefited by this.

The Thessalonians had questions about death and the future. Biblical perspective about that gives you hope and assurance of your future with Christ in eternity. You will not fear death as those who have no hope. And if you like eschatology (prophecy about the end times, especially Jesus' return), you will enjoy Paul's letters to the Thessalonians. As you study Paul's letters to the Thessalonians, you will gain some perspective on the future that God has planned for all believers as well as for human history. One-fourth of 1 Thessalonians and nearly half of 2 Thessalonians deal with the coming of Christ from heaven for His own and the Great Tribulation on earth that will occur afterwards. You will gain perspective on the end times and how to view evil in the present. We will enjoy our time of discovery when we get to those passages.

Knowing the future hope gives you God's perspective on life that you need in your world today. For now, you must live and work in this world. Paul's letters to the Thessalonians have a lot to say about your daily life, including your work. You can view work as worship and see purpose in it when you gain God's perspective.

When you gain the biblical perspective on who God is, what it means to live your life to please Him, and what He has planned for your future, you get a security in Him that allows you to rest and enjoy life today. Who wouldn't want that kind of security? And you will be able to serve God with greater enthusiasm and freedom to impact your world for Him.

3.   In what areas of your life do you need perspective right now?

Respond to the Lord about what you learned today.

DAY TWO STUDY—GET THE BIG PICTURE OF 1 THESSALONIANS

Ask the Lord Jesus to teach you through His Word.

In all of our *Joyful Walk Bible Studies*, we follow the inductive process for Bible Study. The inductive process starts with observation, looking carefully at what the text actually says. *What does the Bible say?* The next step is interpretation, which is trying to understand the author's intended meaning—to him and to the audience who would read or hear it. *What does it mean?* Once you know what the Bible says and what it means, then you are ready for application, which is learning how to live this out in your life. *What application will you make?* When you follow the inductive process for Bible Study, you will be able to confidently dwell in that truth.

What does the Bible say? (This is the "Observation" step in the process of Bible Study.)

Where do we begin? Have you ever heard the saying, "You can't see the forest for the trees?"

The best way to study any book of the Bible is to begin with the "forest" (survey the whole) and then proceed to the "trees" (the individual parts). We will start by getting an overview of what Paul wrote in his letters to the Thessalonians. Since they were written so close together in time, we will read them both this week to get the continuity of thought. We will read them as they were intended—a letter from one dear friend to another.

Today, read the letter called 1 Thessalonians at one sitting. It will take about 12 minutes. You can read the letter in any translation of the Bible you choose. A copy of each letter (NIV translation) is included in this study guide before Lesson One. Feel free to mark anything that grabs your attention, and look for the main topics. Then, answer the questions below.

4. What one thing do you remember most from your reading of this letter?

5. What would you say were the main subjects that Paul covered in this letter?

6. What issues seem to be bothering the Thessalonian church?

7. What questions do you have after reading 1 Thessalonians that you would like to have answered in this study? [Note: You will NOT know when Jesus is coming back. ☺]

Respond to the Lord about what you learned today.

DAY THREE STUDY—GET THE BIG PICTURE OF 2 THESSALONIANS

Ask the Lord Jesus to teach you through His Word.

What does the Bible say? (This is the "Observation" step in the process of Bible Study.)

Today, you will read the letter called 2 Thessalonians at one sitting. It will take about 7 minutes. You can read the letter in any translation of the Bible you choose. A copy of each letter (NIV translation) is included in this study guide before Lesson One. Feel free to mark anything that grabs your attention, and look for repeated topics or phrases. Then, answer the questions below.

8. What subjects did you see in this letter that you also read in 1 Thessalonians?

What does it mean? (This is the "Interpretation" step in the process of Bible Study.)

9. One of the major themes in both letters is the appearing of Christ. We'll cover these verses in more detail as we get to them in the lessons. Right now, read them to get an overview.

- Every chapter of 1 Thessalonians ends with a reference to His appearance. Read 1 Thessalonians 1:9-10; 2:19-20; 3:13; 4:13-17; and 5:23-24. From what you just read, what grabbed your attention?

- In 2 Thessalonians, 18 of the 47 verses deal with future events. Read 2 Thessalonians 1:7-10 and 2:1-2. From what you just read, what grabbed your attention?

10. Another theme shared by 1 and 2 Thessalonians is thankfulness. During difficult times, it is hard to be thankful. Read the following verses and record the reasons Paul found to thank God.

- 1 Thessalonians 1:2-3—

- 1 Thessalonians 2:13—

- 1 Thessalonians 3:9—

- 1 Thessalonians 5:18—

- 2 Thessalonians 1:3-4—

- 2 Thessalonians 2:13-14—

Focus on the Meaning: Firstfruits referred to the beginning of a harvest. All those first century believers were firstfruits of the gospel. We are part of the rest of the harvest.

What application will you make to gain perspective? (This is the "Application" step in the process of Bible Study.)

11. As Paul found reasons to thank God in the midst of very challenging times, you can do the same. Write several reasons that you can be thankful today.

Respond to the Lord about what you learned today. Ask God to show you answers to your questions and what He wants you to learn through this study of 1 and 2 Thessalonians.

Recommended: Listen to the podcast "Start with Knowing and Trusting God" after doing this lesson to reinforce what you have learned. Use the listener guide on the next page.

Start with Knowing and Trusting God

All the references to the end times in the Thessalonian letters are like red threads in needlework. They stand out like crazy. But the softer color of thankfulness tones down the anticipation, impatience, and uncertainty of waiting for Jesus to come back and straighten out this mess on earth. Thankfulness sharpens your focus to see who God is and what He is doing now.

THANKFULNESS REQUIRES KNOWING THE LIVING AND TRUE GOD.

Knowing who God is.

- What is God like? There's a lot of junk out there about God. And your view of God strongly influences your faith in Him.

- That's why it's so important to really get to know the God of the Bible. God's greatness is far beyond human understanding. But the Bible reveals to us part of the picture. We can know Him through what is revealed by Him and about Him. You can know Him.

  - ✓ God is sovereign. He rules over His creation with supreme authority and power, including the affairs of humans.
  - ✓ God is more powerful than anything or anyone else in the entire universe. He is present everywhere at the same time, and He knows everything there is to know.
  - ✓ God is holy and just. He is always set apart from evil, and He works righteousness and justice for all.
  - ✓ God is compassionate and gracious, slow to anger, abounding in love. God's love is patient, kind, forgiving and considers what is best for the one being loved.
  - ✓ God is good. He is good in the tough times, in different ways for each person, and in what He allows or does not allow into our lives.

- Much of the New Testament assumes you know these truths about our God. Paul's letters built on that foundation of truth so that Christians could really know the living and true God.

  *I keep asking that ...the glorious Father, may give you the spirit of wisdom and revelation, so that you may **know him better**. (Ephesians 1:17)*

- We will never know all there is to know about God. There'll always be some mystery about Him. But there's plenty enough revealed in the Bible that we can know Him truthfully, especially in the Gospels. Jesus revealed God to us. Jesus is God in human flesh. He said, *"When you see me, you see God (John 5:19; 14:9-10)."* Every character quality of God is present in Jesus. You can study all the "I Am" statements in the Gospel of John and see this. Jesus brings our God to light so we can know the living and true God.

- As we work through these two letters, we are not just looking for the facts. But we want to know who this glorious Father God is who gives us our identity and purpose in His Son Jesus Christ. Then, the Holy Spirit uses that Scripture to teach us about our God and to give us an intimate awareness of His presence. He is an awesome God!

Knowing what He says

- Knowing what God says is important. You have to start by considering the Bible as being sufficient on its own. It does not need our "improvement." In it, we find what our God considers right and wrong across all time periods, all nationalities, all cultures, and all levels of civilization. In it, we find what our God thinks about us, who we are in His mind and in His plans. We recognize how much we are loved by Him.

- In this Bible Study, we start off each lesson by having you look at the biblical text. What is God saying to us? It's written for us to know, understand, and obey. God gives us plenty of truth in the Bible that we can know and trust.

Knowing God through trusting Him with something

- In 1 and 2 Thessalonians, we'll see evidence of what it looks like to trust God with someone or something important to you and then watch what He does. There are two aspects to trusting God.
    - ✓ First aspect: Trusting God while you do your part His way. To do your part His way involves your knowing what His way is.
    - ✓ Second aspect: Trusting Him to do His part alongside what you are doing. You have to trust God to work in the background of life and to make things happen in those areas over which you have no direct access.

KNOWING AND TRUSTING GOD LEAD TO THANKFULNESS.

- As our hearts become intimately acquainted with our amazing, personal God, we can hardly do anything but be thankful. When you have trusted God with something, and you look back to see what He did, how can you not be thankful? That's why it's so important to record how God has been faithful to you. *Malachi 3:16*

- In all of Paul's letters, we can see that Paul trusted God with the welfare of his new converts and the newly established churches. So he started off nearly every letter with thanks to God for the people themselves and for what God had done in their lives. He expressed thankfulness for his own suffering and difficult circumstances because of what God taught him through it.

- When you stop and think about who God is and what He has done in your life and in the lives of those you love, you can always find reasons to be thankful. The biblical perspective on life leads to thankfulness.

Let Jesus satisfy your heart with His perspective on life in the present and in the future. Then, live securely in Him during this time of waiting.

2: Perspective on the Gospel

1 Thessalonians 1:1-10

DAY ONE STUDY—GET THE BIG PICTURE

What does the Bible say? (This is the "Observation" step of Bible Study.)

Let's start digging into this wonderful letter from God to us. For every lesson, we will begin with reading the whole passage to get the big picture before we study the verses more closely.

Ask the Lord Jesus to teach you through His Word.

Read the Bible passage below (NIV). Use your own method (colored pencils, lines, shapes) to mark 1) anything that grabs your attention, 2) words you want to understand, and 3) anything repeated in this passage. Draw arrows between thoughts that connect.

1 *Paul, Silas and Timothy,*

To the church of the Thessalonians in God the Father and the Lord Jesus Christ:

Grace and peace to you.

2 We always thank God for all of you and continually mention you in our prayers. 3 We remember before our God and Father your work produced by faith, your labor prompted by love, and your endurance inspired by hope in our Lord Jesus Christ.

4 For we know, brothers and sisters loved by God, that he has chosen you, 5 because our gospel came to you not simply with words but also with power, with the Holy Spirit and deep conviction. You know how we lived among you for your sake. 6 You became imitators of us and of the Lord, for you welcomed the message in the midst of severe suffering with the joy given by the Holy Spirit. 7 And so you became a model to all the believers in Macedonia and Achaia. 8 The Lord's message rang out from you not only in Macedonia and Achaia—your faith in God has become known everywhere. Therefore we do not need to say anything about it, 9 for they themselves report what kind of reception you gave us. They tell how you turned to God from idols to serve the living and true God, 10 and to wait for his Son from heaven, whom he raised from the dead—Jesus, who rescues us from the coming wrath.

1. What grabbed your attention from vv. 1-10?

2. What verses or specific words do you want to understand better?

3. What words or phrases are repeated in this passage? Give verses.

4. ***Gain perspective:*** From this lesson's passage (1:1-10), choose one verse to dwell upon all week long. Write it in the space below. Ask God to teach you through this verse.

Respond to the Lord about what He's shown you today.

DAY TWO STUDY

Read 1 Thessalonians 1:1-10. Ask the Lord Jesus to teach you through His Word.

What does it mean? (This is the "Interpretation" step of Bible Study.)

Today, we will focus on vv. 1-8. We'll cover vv. 9-10 in the Day Three Study.

5. Look at vv. 1-2. This is called the "salutation." In ancient letters, the salutation included both the letter writer and the recipient's name.

   • The letter was from Paul. Who was with Paul?

   • Who were the recipients?

   From the Greek: "Silvanus" was the Roman (Latin) form of his name, which Paul preferred over "Silas," the Jewish (Aramaic) form. Luke used "Silas" (Acts 15:22). Silas and Timothy were Paul's primary associates on his second missionary journey, during which the church at Thessalonica came into existence (Acts 15:40). (*Dr. Constable's Notes on 1 Thessalonians 2020 Edition*, p. 11)

6. Paul usually began his letters with the greeting "grace and peace to you." Grace (Greek, *charis*) was a common greeting among the Greeks, and peace (Hebrew, "shalom") was a common greeting among Jews. Paul combined them together, elevating their meaning. Read Romans 5:1-2. What is the connection between these two words?

7. Although no church is perfect, there are definite marks of maturity Paul emphasized when commending a church. What characteristics of this church does Paul commend in v. 3?

Scriptural Insight: Three characteristics of these Christians stood out to Paul: First, they had turned to Christ in "faith." Second, they had served Him out of "love." Third, they had borne up under tribulation patiently, because of the "hope" that lay before them. [Each of these] found its object in Jesus Christ as they lived before God. They had exercised faith in the past when they first trusted Christ. They were loving Him in the present, and they were hoping for His return in the future. (*Dr. Constable's Notes on 2 Corinthians 2020 Edition,* pp. 13-14)

8. In vv. 4-5, what assurances did Paul give to the Thessalonians about their faith (vv. 4-5)?

9. In vv. 6-8, we see evidence of their faith, love, and hope in Christ.

    *   Whom have the Thessalonians chosen to imitate (v. 6) and how?

    *   By doing so, what have they become to others (v. 7)?

    *   What was the result (v. 8, first part)?

From the Greek: The word *exechetai*, translated "rang out" (NIV), could be rendered "reverberated" like an echo that keeps on going. Paul saw the Thessalonians as amplifiers or relay stations that not only received the gospel message but sent it farther on its way with increased power and scope...The Thessalonians had acted as relay runners by passing the gospel they had heard on to farther places. They may have been a missionary church. (*The Bible Knowledge Commentary New Testament,* p. 692; *Dr. Constable's Notes on 1 Thessalonians 2020 Edition,* p. 16)

10. What principles should be guiding us in imitating others?

- 1 Corinthians 11:1—

- Ephesians 5:1-2—

- 1 Timothy 4:12—

Think About It: In 1 Corinthians 11:1, Paul says, "Follow my example, as I follow the example of Christ." That's the kind of statement that gets the apostle Paul slapped with labels like "arrogant" and "egotistical." Maybe that bothers you, too. Why didn't Paul just take himself out of the equation and tell people to follow Christ? The answer is that Paul knew we all need a role model, a picture of Christ that makes the heart, mind and ways of Christ visible and tangible. To step into a role of leadership is essentially to state, "Follow me as I follow Christ." If people are going to follow us, our primary task is to lead ourselves well ... The first step toward leading yourself well is following well ... And if you are a Christ follower, the practice of following [Him] well is fundamental to your identity and may be one of the greatest tests of your character. (Heather Zempel, *Community Is Messy*, pages 67-68)

What application will you make to gain a biblical perspective?

11. In the gospels, we see that Jesus would connect with people and impart truth to them. And He has used His servants to reach you and model for you how to follow Him.

- Who are the earthly examples who have demonstrated to you how to follow Christ well?

- In whom are you consciously investing right now so that they would learn how to follow Christ by imitating you? What results have you seen in their lives?

Respond to the Lord about what you learned today.

DAY THREE STUDY

Read 1 Thessalonians 1:1-10. Ask the Lord Jesus to teach you through His Word.

What does it mean?

Today, we will focus on vv. 9-10.

> **Historical Insight:** The fact that God is a living Person was precious to the Jews and to Paul; this is the characteristic by which God is most often distinguished from so-called gods in the Old Testament. He is the only living God; all other gods are not alive and therefore not worthy objects of worship. (*The Bible Knowledge Commentary New Testament,* p. 692)

12. Verse 9 gives us the perfect definition of repentance—to change one's mind and, therefore, one's direction in life. The Thessalonians are telling their own story of repentance. What change did they make?

> **Focus on the Meaning:** The repentance followed the turning to God. It didn't precede it. When they turned to God, they automatically turned from idols. Take your hand and hold it so the palm of your hand is facing toward you. Now turn your hand around. When you turned your hand around, the back side of your hand now faces you, and the palm of your hand automatically turned away from you. Just so, you cannot turn to Christ Jesus without turning from something, my friend. That turning from something is repentance. It was not reformation first and faith in Christ second, but it was faith in Christ first with the result that idols were forsaken. (*Dr. Constable's Notes on 1 Thessalonians 2020 Edition*, p. 18)

13. The Thessalonians were mostly pagan Gentiles who may have only heard about the Jewish God before Paul came to town. And their lives had been steeped in the functions of idol worship. Considering their likely previous habits and pursuits, how could their change of mind and direction (v. 9) have impacted their daily lives? Look elsewhere in vv. 3-8 for evidence of the changes.

14. Another aspect of our faith is waiting for Jesus' return (v. 10). Write what Paul tells them in the space below.

Historical Insight: … the formerly pagan Thessalonians probably understood the [appearing] of Christ in terms of the visits of the imperial rulers of Rome. These rulers were increasingly being thought of as the manifestations of deities who required elaborate ceremonies and honors when they visited the various cities of the Empire. (*Dr. Constable's Notes on 1 Thessalonians 2020 Edition,* pp. 34-35)

15. What evidence do we have that Jesus is indeed returning? See Mark 13:26-27; Luke 21:27-28; and Acts 1:11.

Scriptural Insight: Paul speaks often in these two letters about Jesus' coming. We'll see more in 1 Thessalonians 2:19; 3:13; 4:16-17; 2 Thessalonians 1:7; and 2:1.

16. When Jesus appears, He will rescue us from what?

What is God's wrath?

When you read or hear about God's wrath, do you picture God raging with out-of-control anger? Since that is our experience with human anger, we might think that His is the same, only bigger. But the Bible teaches that God's wrath is not a mood or a fit of temper. God's disposition toward sin and evil is as constant and unrelenting as His love and goodness. He hates and rejects evil in a perfect and holy anger. He will never bend or compromise with it. His own nature demands that He judge it through action.

Why does God do this? He loves His creation. He desires it to reflect His holiness. To preserve His creation, God must destroy whatever would destroy it. Every wrathful judgment of God is and will be a holy act of preservation.

Let's put this in everyday terms that you and I can understand. How much do you hate germs like the flu virus infiltrating your home? Do you use a disinfectant to clean with gusto and keep your family from getting sick? My disposition toward the flu virus (or worse) is wrath. It is pollution of my home. I do whatever is necessary to get rid of it. Don't you?

Consider ants in your house. You probably do not invite ants into your house and just ignore their presence while they take over your kitchen or bedroom. Don't you do whatever you can to attack their presence and restore your home to a safe environment for yourself and your family? When I spray ant killer where I've seen ants crawling in my kitchen, I am expressing wrath against their destruction of my safe home environment.

God's wrath is far more serious, of course. Sin is much more awful with far more destructive consequences than the flu virus or ants. But you get the idea.

Our culture tends to dismiss the seriousness of human sinfulness. We blame people and circumstances for our behavior and attitudes rather than blaming our deceitful, desperately wicked hearts. God hates sin. It incurs His anger. But God loves people. God's holy wrath against all sin is fully satisfied by Jesus' sacrifice on the cross. The term used to describe that in the Bible is *propitiation* (pronounced like initiation). Because of what Jesus did on the cross, God extends mercy to everyone who believes in Christ. That means God is satisfied…no longer angry at your sin, and His wrath against sin is no longer directed at you. This is truth for you to know and claim.

17. Read John 3:36; Romans 5:9; and 2 Thessalonians 1:7-10. According to these verses,

- Who will experience God's wrath and why?

- Who will not experience God's wrath and why?

- What is the one sin that keeps anyone from experiencing the wonderful salvation of God?

Belief, not behavior, is the basis for determining who receives eternal life and salvation from God's wrath. As a believer in Christ, you are saved from God's wrath and eternally lavished in His love instead.

What application will you make to gain a biblical perspective?

18. We said that repentance means to change one's mind and, therefore, one's direction in life.

- When you first believed, what changes took place in your mind?

- How has your life altered (change of direction) since you encountered the living and true God? Consider using a creative means (poem, song, drawing, prayer) to illustrate what has happened to your life since encountering the living and true God.

Respond to the Lord about what you learned in this lesson.

Recommended: Listen to the podcast "Spread the Light of the Gospel" after doing this lesson to reinforce what you have learned. Use the listener guide on the next page.

Spread the Light of the Gospel

God calls us out of darkness into His wonderful light. And He uses us as light-bearers to declare His faithfulness and lead other people to Him. We are God's dearly loved children who can be light-bearers to anyone still living in darkness.

UNBELIEVERS LIVE IN THE KINGDOM OF DARKNESS.

- Every human being born on this planet is born into bondage to the kingdom of darkness, regardless of where you live or how much money and status you have.

- We have an enemy who likes to keep us in that bondage.

  The god of this age has blinded the minds of unbelievers, so that they cannot see the light of the gospel that displays the glory of Christ, who is the image of God. (2 Corinthians 4:4).

- But our God has done something to rescue us from that darkness. He sent Jesus. Jesus is the light to overcome the darkness. *John 8:12*

- Our God wanted to open our eyes and turn us from darkness to light, and from the power of Satan to God. Light reaching into the kingdom of darkness. *Acts 26:17-18; 2 Corinthians 4:6*

- You and I are chosen to be God's mouthpiece to the world around us.

  You [Christians] are ... a people belonging to God, that you may declare the praises of him who called you out of darkness into his wonderful light. (1 Peter 2:9)

- We are to share with the world that the light has come to rescue people from the one who wants everyone to stay blind, living in the kingdom of darkness. The Thessalonians spread the message of God's wonderful light.

THE LORD'S MESSAGE RINGS OUT.

  *The Lord's message **rang out** from you not only in Macedonia and Achaia—your faith in God has become known everywhere. (1 Thessalonians 1:8)*

- "The word of the Lord" refers to the gospel. It comes to us from the Lord, not from any human religious philosopher or theologian. It centers on the Lord Jesus, who gave Himself on the cross for our sins. So we can ring it out securely to others.

- The word picture used in 1 Thessalonians 1:8 is like a relay station that not only received the gospel message but sent it farther on its way with increased power and scope. Or it's like relay runners who took the gospel they had heard and passed it on to farther places.

DECLARE WHAT HE HAS DONE.

- As people walk around in their blindness-darkness, they are groping along the walls to find their way to a door that will free them from their fear and give them purpose in life. God's plan to meet that need for every woman and every man is a relationship with Himself through faith in His Son Jesus Christ.

- Our God sent His Son Jesus into the world to lead the way out of the darkness. But He chooses to use us—headstrong, messy people—to be his light-bearers to the blind and to ring out His message of love to fearful people on this earth.

- We are the light-bearers. We communicate to those around us who are enshrouded in darkness that God is real and available to anyone who wants Him. That's the good news. That is "The Gospel."

THE GOSPEL IS THE GOOD NEWS ABOUT JESUS CHRIST.

- The Gospel is the good news about Jesus Christ coming to earth to save us from our sins. Christianity is Christ! It's all about a relationship with Him.

  "Jesus Christ **laid down** His life **for** you so that He could **give** His life **to** you so that He could **live** His life **through** you." (Major Ian Thomas, *The Saving Life of Christ*)

- If you have opportunity to tell someone one thing, tell her about Jesus.
  - ✓ Tell her that God loves her and wants a relationship with her. But sin separates her from having a relationship with God.
  - ✓ Tell her that Jesus is God, who came to earth as a man, and died for her sins.
  - ✓ Tell her that she can be completely forgiven of her sins and receive eternal life with God simply by believing in Jesus as her Savior.

Let the music of the gospel sound forth from you. Spread its light.

The light shines in the darkness, and the darkness has not overcome it. (John 1:5)

Let Jesus satisfy your heart with His perspective on life in the present and in the future. Then, live securely in Him during this time of waiting.

3: Perspective on Being a Servant-Leader

1 Thessalonians 2:1-12

DAY ONE STUDY—GET THE BIG PICTURE

Ask the Lord Jesus to teach you through His Word.

What does the Bible say?

Read the Bible passage below (NIV) including verses from the last lesson. Use your own method (colored pencils, lines, shapes) to mark 1) anything that grabs your attention, 2) words you want to understand, and 3) topics you have seen before in this letter. Draw arrows between thoughts that connect.

1 *[8] The Lord's message rang out from you not only in Macedonia and Achaia—your faith in God has become known everywhere. Therefore we do not need to say anything about it, [9] for they themselves report what kind of reception you gave us. They tell how you turned to God from idols to serve the living and true God, [10] and to wait for his Son from heaven, whom he raised from the dead—Jesus, who rescues us from the coming wrath.*

2 *You know, brothers and sisters, that our visit to you was not without results. [2] We had previously suffered and been treated outrageously in Philippi, as you know, but with the help of our God we dared to tell you his gospel in the face of strong opposition. [3] For the appeal we make does not spring from error or impure motives, nor are we trying to trick you. [4] On the contrary, we speak as those approved by God to be entrusted with the gospel. We are not trying to please people but God, who tests our hearts. [5] You know we never used flattery, nor did we put on a mask to cover up greed—God is our witness. [6] We were not looking for praise from people, not from you or anyone else, even though as apostles of Christ we could have asserted our authority. [7] Instead, we were like young children among you.*

Just as a nursing mother cares for her children, [8] so we cared for you. Because we loved you so much, we were delighted to share with you not only the gospel of God but our lives as well. [9] Surely you remember, brothers and sisters, our toil and hardship; we worked night and day in order not to be a burden to anyone while we preached the gospel of God to you. [10] You are witnesses, and so is God, of how holy, righteous and blameless we were among you who believed. [11] For you know that we dealt with each of you as a father deals with his own children, [12] encouraging, comforting and urging you to live lives worthy of God, who calls you into his kingdom and glory.

1. What grabbed your attention from these verses?

2. What verses or specific words do you want to understand better?

3. What words or phrases are repeated in this passage? Give verses.

4. What topics (if any) in this passage have we studied in previous lessons?

5. **Gain perspective:** From this lesson's passage (2:1-12), choose one verse to dwell upon all week long. Write it in the space below. Ask God to teach you through this verse.

Respond to the Lord about what you learned today.

DAY TWO STUDY

Read 1 Thessalonians 2:1-12. Ask the Lord Jesus to teach you through His Word.

What does it mean?

Today, we will focus on vv. 1-6.

6. Paul followed Christ in both teaching and example of what it means to be a servant-leader. His words in 1 Thessalonians chapter 2 are evidence of that. Read Mark 10:42-45. How did Jesus distinguish the difference between worldly leaders and what He wants for His followers to do?

7. A servant-leader knows who is really the one in authority. Paul repeatedly stressed that the message he preached had greater authority than being from Paul.

   - To whom does the gospel message belong (vv. 2, 8, 9)?

   - What is the gospel message with which they were entrusted (v. 4)? Read 1 Corinthians 15:1-5 and John 3:16.

8. Paul referenced a specific event in 1 Thessalonians 2:2. Read Acts 16:16-40. What happened that could have discouraged Paul and Silas from continuing their mission but didn't stop them?

The common reaction to unpopular messages, then and now, is this: "If you can't refute the message, attack the messenger." That seems to have been the situation in Thessalonica. Someone was spreading rumors to slander the character of Paul and his companions and their motives for coming to Thessalonica. Paul's defense was to remind them of the truth of his conduct while in their midst.

9. What did Paul and his team **not** do when proclaiming the gospel (vv. 3-6)? See also 2 Corinthians 4:2.

> **Focus on the Meaning:** "To trick" referred to the use of a lure for catching fish. The phrase was commonly used in Paul's day for any cunning intended to gain a profit. (*NIV Study Bible*, p. 1821)

10. In contrast, what did Paul and his team do whenever they proclaimed the gospel (vv. 4-6)? See also 1 Corinthians 2:4-5.

From the Greek: The phrase in 1 Thessalonians 2:4, "approved by God to be entrusted with the Gospel," literally means "found to have stood the test."

11. Paul lived and worked to please whom (v. 4)? Why? See also 2 Corinthians 5:9.

Scriptural Insight: Paul claimed that his message was true, his motives were pure, and his methods were straightforward. He and his companions had behaved in Thessalonica as they had elsewhere, as faithful servants of God. They did not preach for the approval of "men," but of "God," who scrutinizes motives. (*Dr. Constable's Notes on 1 Thessalonians 2020 Edition,* p. 24)

The Christian sports ministry, Athletes in Action, teaches college and professional athletes to play for an "Audience of One." The intent of the phrase is to help Christian players remember that everywhere in life—even in a stadium full of people—we are to live to please God, not men. The same is true of every Christian in any part of life. We live for an Audience of One—to the glory of God, not of ourselves. A Christian servant-leader always keeps in mind the "Audience of One."

What application will you make to gain a biblical perspective?

12. Have you been slandered by someone in order to keep people from listening to or respecting you? How did you respond? How should you respond and why? See also 1 Peter 2:15.

13. Just as Paul, we are called to be faithful to God and to please Him and not men. If you choose to do everything in life for an "Audience of One,"

- What changes do you need to make in your thinking and behavior?

- What gets in your way of doing this? Where is your greatest struggle to please God more than pleasing people?

- How can we help one another to faithfully live for an "Audience of One?"

Respond to the Lord about what you learned today.

DAY THREE STUDY

Read 1 Thessalonians 2:1-12. Ask the Lord Jesus to teach you through His Word.

What does it mean?

Today, we will focus on vv. 7-12.

14. Once again, let's look at Jesus' teaching about being a servant-leader. Read John 13:13-17. What do you learn from his example and words?

15. Serving others usually requires sacrifice of time, energy, and possessions. This is certainly true of women and men who serve as mothers and fathers to children. Paul, Timothy and Silas took on the roles of both mother and father to their spiritual children in Thessalonica.

- How did they serve as a "mother" to them?

- How did they serve as a "father" to them?

- What did they **not** do to their audience (vv. 6, 9)?

Historical Insight: In the Greco-Roman period in which he lived, philosophers like Paul were highly valued and in high job demand. A philosopher of his day could earn income in one of 3 acceptable ways. They could charge fees for their teaching (Acts 19:9; 2 Corinthians 11). They could serve rich families as a kind of 'house philosopher' to educate the head of household & his children. Or they could work at a tradecraft while carrying on philosophical discussions with co-workers and members of the general public who visited the workshop. That would be the equivalent social setting of a coffee shop today. This last option was Paul's method of financially supporting himself as needed. From an early age, Paul received skill training in what is believed to be his family's business of tent-making (also, leather-working). It's easy to imagine Paul yakking away, teaching others while keeping busy with his hands. Ministry was never meant to be separated from work. (Ron Newton, *Lessons from Crunch Time Business in the Bible*)

16. *Deeper Discoveries (optional):*

- There are a number of biblical examples of nursing mothers and the value of nursing relationships in the sight of God. Read Numbers 11:12; 1 Samuel 1:21-24; Psalm 8:2 and Matthew 21:16; Psalm 131:2; Isaiah 40:11; 49:14-15; and 66:7-13. What do you learn?

- The Bible also used a baby's need for milk as a spiritual teaching tool. Read 1 Corinthians 3:1-2; Hebrews 5:12-14; and 1 Peter 2:1-3. What do you learn?

17. One of the accusations Paul faced in several of his churches centered around how he differed from the usual professional speakers who traveled from town to town, entertained the crowds, and expected the listeners to pay for their "wisdom." Itinerant philosophers and orators were common in the Roman Empire. [Note: Greek culture considered manual labor such as Paul's tent-making to be "lower class."]

- Was it wrong for Paul to preach the gospel free of charge?

- What reason did Paul give for choosing to humbly serve the Thessalonians like that?

- What ultimately is Paul's goal (v. 12)?

- How were his actions an application of Jesus' words in Mark 10:42-45 and John 13:13-16?

Scriptural Insight: Paul's principle was to preach and teach without charging those who benefited directly from his ministry. This is a good policy in church planting, but it is not normative for a settled pastoral ministry (1 Corinthians 9:14; 1 Timothy 5:17-18). (*Dr. Constable's Notes on 2 Corinthians 2020 Edition,* p. 152)

18. The kingdom referenced in v. 12 would be the millennial kingdom Jesus would set up at His Second Coming to earth (Revelation 20). [Note: the "Extra Lesson" at the end of this study guide covers this in more detail.] Why or how would looking ahead to the bliss of being in that kingdom be an incentive for godly living now?

19. Paul had come to Thessalonica to give, not to get. He gave himself and his message to the Thessalonians out of love for them, not for personal gain. Four times, he wrote "you know" (1:5; 2:2, 5, 6) reminding them of what they had witnessed with their own eyes. From vv. 1-12, we have a beautiful, clear presentation of the heart attitude of a "servant-leader" representing Christ. Summarize what you learn from these verses.

   Think About It: Such behavior displayed toward people should shut the mouths of any critics.

20. ***Deeper Discoveries (optional):*** Read John 10:1-13. It is common in the Bible for kings and priests and other leaders to be considered "shepherds" of the people who are "their sheep." Discuss the distinction between true shepherds who are servant-leaders and those who are not serving their sheep.

What application will you make to gain a biblical perspective?

21. All of us have spheres of authority. As a servant-leader belonging to and representing Christ, we are to use our authority for building up those in our sphere of influence.

   • Some of us don't handle that authority well. What is your heart attitude towards those you serve? Do you struggle with being bossy and bearing down on others within your sphere of influence? Where do you need to improve?

- Our God is the giver of every good and perfect gift (James 1:17) and can produce such a servant-leader's heart in you if you seek it. Ask the Lord to teach you graciousness, gentleness, and give you a servant's heart for those in your sphere of influence (home, work, neighborhood, church). You can say, "Lord Jesus, I can't do this on my own. But you can do this in me and through me. I will trust you to show me how." Then, watch what He does!

Respond to the Lord about what you learned today.

Recommended: Listen to the podcast "Gain Biblical Perspective on Leadership" after doing this lesson to reinforce what you have learned. Use the listener guide on the next page.

Gain Biblical Perspective on Leadership

All believers are united into the Body of Christ—the Church. The Church as the Body of Christ is not an organization but something living. It transcends all cultures, languages, national boundaries, and time periods. Knowing we are part of this unity gives us radically different reasons for behaving well in our relationships with one another. What each of us does can affect positively or negatively the other members of this organism, the universal Body of Christ represented to us in our local church body. We are to preserve and encourage that fellowship among all believers produced by the Spirit who is indwelling each of us.

But this calls for a radical lifestyle, opposite of the "it's all about me" our western culture teaches. It's not all about me. It's not all about you. It's all about God. Our goal in life is to please God.

LIVING FOR AN AUDIENCE OF ONE

- Our mindset should be that we have an Audience of One. We are to live to please God, not humans. We live for an Audience of One—to the glory of God not of ourselves.

- Jesus is the one who demonstrated for us how to serve one another, especially in a leadership role. He demonstrated how a leader is to serve rather than be served. *Mark 10:42-45*

- Anyone in authority should be a servant-leader to those they are leading. Jesus demonstrated what He meant by that throughout His ministry and in His death on the cross. But He gave His followers a visual picture of what it means to be a servant-leader. *John 13:13-17*

FOLLOWING JESUS' EXAMPLE TO BE A SERVANT-LEADER INVOLVES CHOICES

Choice #1. Think of others before yourself.

> *Do nothing out of selfish ambition or vain conceit. Rather, in humility value others above yourselves, not looking to your own interests but each of you to the interests of the others. (Philippians 2:3-4)*

- In 1 Thessalonians chapter 2, Paul repeatedly emphasized that he and his team did nothing out of selfish ambition or vain conceit. They only did what was good for those to whom he was sharing the gospel and his life as well.

- Jesus had privileges as God, but He did not consider His equality with God as something to hold onto selfishly. He thought of us and our needs. He did this so we didn't have to continue living selfish lives. He has enabled us to be others-oriented.

Choice #2. Serve out of love and worship for God.

- Our service is to be an extension of the worship we render to God. *Romans 12:1*

- God dwells in people. So there is no sacred/secular division in any Christian woman's life. What you do at church is no more sacred service than what you do at home, at school, or at work. Everything you do is service to God within His temple, which is your body.

- Remember that the focus of serving is not to earn favor with God or with people.

Choice #3. Willingly sacrifice as you serve.

- Jesus sacrificed Himself for us. His body, His reputation, His time, and His glory. Serving others usually costs something. Time, money, mental energy, physical work.

- The difference between sacrifice and suffering: Suffering is usually imposed on you by someone or something else. Sacrifice is something you are willing to give through time, money, skills, and physical labor without whining or complaining. Paul willingly sacrificed for the Thessalonians as his spiritual children.

Choice #4. Glorify God more than yourself as you lead.

- Jesus glorified God. Paul, as a servant-leader, declared his goal was teaching people to live lives worthy of God, not him. His goal was for God to be glorified. That will lead to pleasing one another if God's glory is the goal of everyone involved. *1 Thessalonians 2:12*

- We are living, breathing, walking, talking representatives of the living God. They are watching us. We are living letters to the world around us. They are reading us. We are telling the truth about who God is by the way we live as well as by what we say.

- To live is Christ means to live **as** Christ, which means to let Christ live His life through you. The world sees Him through you. And that glorifies God. *Philippians 1:21*

Serving one another is not the main goal. Letting Christ live His life through us as we serve is the main goal. Serving one another is the means. Serving Jesus is from the heart, not a task. It means you willingly sacrifice and don't whine about it. Be the best servant-leader you can be for your Audience of One—the Lord Jesus Christ. He showed us how. Choose to do it His way!

Let Jesus satisfy your heart with His perspective on life in the present and in the future. Then, live securely in Him during this time of waiting.

4: Perspective on Suffering

1 Thessalonians 2:13-20

DAY ONE STUDY—GET THE BIG PICTURE

Ask the Lord Jesus to teach you through His Word.

What does the Bible say?

Read the Bible passage below (NIV) including verses from the last lesson. Use your own method (colored pencils, lines, shapes) to mark 1) anything that grabs your attention, 2) words you want to understand, and 3) topics you have seen before in this letter. Draw arrows between thoughts that connect.

2 [7] *Just as a nursing mother cares for her children,* [8] *so we cared for you. Because we loved you so much, we were delighted to share with you not only the gospel of God but our lives as well.* [9] *Surely you remember, brothers and sisters, our toil and hardship; we worked night and day in order not to be a burden to anyone while we preached the gospel of God to you.* [10] *You are witnesses, and so is God, of how holy, righteous and blameless we were among you who believed.* [11] *For you know that we dealt with each of you as a father deals with his own children,* [12] *encouraging, comforting and urging you to live lives worthy of God, who calls you into his kingdom and glory.*

[13] *And we also thank God continually because, when you received the word of God, which you heard from us, you accepted it not as a human word, but as it actually is, the word of God, which is indeed at work in you who believe.* [14] *For you, brothers and sisters, became imitators of God's churches in Judea, which are in Christ Jesus: You suffered from your own people the same things those churches suffered from the Jews* [15] *who killed the Lord Jesus and the prophets and also drove us out. They displease God and are hostile to everyone* [16] *in their effort to keep us from speaking to the Gentiles so that they may be saved. In this way they always heap up their sins to the limit. The wrath of God has come upon them at last.*

[17] *But, brothers and sisters, when we were orphaned by being separated from you for a short time (in person, not in thought), out of our intense longing we made every effort to see you.* [18] *For we wanted to come to you—certainly I, Paul, did, again and again—but Satan blocked our way.* [19] *For what is our hope, our joy, or the crown in which we will glory in the presence of our Lord Jesus when he comes? Is it not you?* [20] *Indeed, you are our glory and joy.*

1. What grabbed your attention from vv. 13-20?

2. What verses or specific words do you want to understand better?

3. What words or phrases are repeated in this passage? Give verses.

4. What topics (if any) in this passage have we studied in previous lessons?

5. *Gain perspective:* From this lesson's passage (2:13-20), choose one verse to dwell upon all week long. Write it in the space below. Ask God to teach you through this verse.

Respond to the Lord about what you learned today.

DAY TWO STUDY

Read 1 Thessalonians 2:13-20. Ask the Lord Jesus to teach you through His Word.

What does it mean?

Today, we will focus on vv. 13-16.

6. Why did Paul thank God (v. 13)?

7. What were the Thessalonians experiencing?

8. True leadership requires the ability to define a situation, attitude, or goal. Followers ask their leader, "What is the best way to think about this situation?"

   • How did Paul answer this question for them (vv. 14-15)?

   • Of what had he reminded them about their suffering in 1:6-7?

   • How would Paul's words be an encouragement to the Thessalonians?

9. The Thessalonians are connected to other churches as part of the Body of Christ and by their suffering. What emotions and reactions often occur when a person is under persecution?

10. Remember that suffering is usually imposed on you by someone or something else and not something you choose to willingly give up. Read the following verses and list the possible "benefits" of persecution or suffering (if any).

    • Matthew 5:10-12—

    • 2 Corinthians 1:6-10—

- 1 Peter 4:12-16, 19—

- James 1:2-4—

11. What specific accusations did Paul make against the opposition in 1 Thessalonians 2:15-16?

Think About It: An unbeliever who is willing to live and let live with respect to personal convictions regarding God is less dangerous than one who not only disbelieves himself but also tries to keep others from hearing the gospel. The unbelieving Jews in Thessalonica were of the latter variety. (*The Bible Knowledge Commentary New Testament,* p. 696)

Paul spoke not just as a recipient of persecution but also as a once active participant. In his personal testimony, he told of how he persecuted Christians to their imprisonment and death (Acts 22:4). In 1 Timothy 1:13, he wrote these words, "Even though I was once a blasphemer and a persecutor and a violent man, I was shown mercy because I acted in ignorance and unbelief."

12. Read Romans 9:1-5 and 10:1. Did Paul's condemnation of those Jews come from personal hatred towards them? Explain your answer. What was his (and God's) desire for all people?

Scriptural Insight: Paul desperately wanted unbelieving Jews to come to faith in Christ (Rom. 9:1-3; 10:1). Yet they were some of his most antagonistic persecutors (cf. 2 Cor. 11:24, 26). Their actions were "not pleasing to God" (an understatement), and were not in the best interests of all men who needed to hear the gospel ... By their opposition, these enemies of the gospel added more transgressions on their own heads ("always fill up the measure of their sins"), with the result that they hastened God's judgment ("wrath") of them (cf. Gen. 15:16). They not only rejected the gospel themselves, but they also discouraged others from accepting it. (*Dr. Constable's Notes on 1 Thessalonians 2020 Edition,* p. 29)

What application will you make to gain a biblical perspective?

13. Review what you learned in Question 10 about the benefits of suffering.

- *Regarding persecution:* In what ways do you experience suffering related to being a Christian? What benefits have you seen God bring from such suffering that gives you encouragement?

- *Regarding general suffering:* In what ways do you experience suffering other than persecution for your faith? What benefits have you seen God bring from such suffering that gives you encouragement?

Respond to the Lord about what you learned today.

DAY THREE STUDY

Read 1 Thessalonians 2:13-20. Ask the Lord Jesus to teach you through His Word.

What does it mean?

Today, we will focus on vv. 17-20.

14. Paul refers to being "torn away" or "orphaned" from them. The meaning of the original Greek word used here is "to be bereaved of a parent or parents." It was sudden, not of his own choosing. In what terms had Paul already expressed a "family" relationship to them?

15. Read Acts 17:5-15 to see how he was torn away from the Thessalonians. In 1 Thessalonians 2:18, Paul blames Satan for blocking him from revisiting the Thessalonians. From Acts 17:6-9, what was one possible way Satan hindered Paul from returning? (Think legal!)

Scriptural Insight: The word translated "blocked" or "hindered" means to make a road impassable like a flood sweeping out a bridge or the roadbed. It also means to place an obstacle sharply in the path to detain a person unnecessarily. Paul's reason for deciding to return was to provide additional spiritual help for the new converts. This in itself is clearly the will of God in any situation. Seen as such, any hindrance becomes opposition to the will of God. Regardless of who was involved on the human level, the ultimate leader of this kind of opposition is Satan. (*The Bible Knowledge Commentary New Testament,* p. 697)

16. Even if he couldn't legally return to see them yet, what could he still do? See 1 Thessalonians 1:1 and 3:2.

17. Jesus knew the reality of Satan at work in the world to hinder people from believing in God. Discuss Jesus' comments in John 8:37-44 in light of what Paul experienced in Thessalonica.

18. Of what importance were the Thessalonians to Paul (vv. 19-20)? See also 2:8, 11.

From the Greek: In this context, the crown (Gr. *stephanos*) to which Paul was referring was not a royal crown but a wreath used on festive occasions. It also denoted a token of public honor for distinguished service.

19. Of what was Paul confident about Jesus (v. 19)?

20. In what would Paul glory in the presence of Jesus? Why is this important for us to know and remember?

Scriptural Insight: They were everything that was worth anything to Paul. They were his hope as he watched them grow into maturity. They were his joy as he thought about what they used to be and what they had become and would be by the grace of God. They were his crown as a symbol of God's blessing on his life and work. (*The Bible Knowledge Commentary New Testament,* p. 697)

What application will you make to gain a biblical perspective?

21. Have you been torn away from someone you love? What steps are you able to take to sustain and nurture the relationship? How are you trusting God until you can be with them again?

22. Consider what or whom will be your glory at the end of your earthly life. Is it being great at your work or the people you have influenced? If you tend to value your work (career, accomplishments, status) more than people, ask the Lord to change your heart and your priorities so that the influence on people in your life will become more important to you than your work. That is His will so He will answer that prayer.

Respond to the Lord about what you learned today.

Recommended: Listen to the podcast "Gain the Biblical Perspective from the Bible" after doing this lesson to reinforce what you have learned. Use the listener guide on the next page.

Gain the Biblical Perspective from the Bible

Once you have turned from all your idols and trusted in the living God, the Holy Spirit moves into your spirit and begins to teach you the truth of God. Then you need wisdom to know what to do with that information. Wisdom is "smartness" gained through the experience of making right or good decisions and avoiding the wrong or bad ones.

WISDOM BEGINS WITH THE WORD OF GOD.

- The Bible teaches that wisdom is directly related to your acceptance of and obedience to God's Word. *1 Thessalonians 2:13*

- Like the Bereans in Acts 17, when listening to someone teach the Scriptures, open your Bible and check it out.

- There are some who make it their goal to keep us from knowing God's truth and gaining the biblical perspective on life. That's why perspective on any subject or issue of life should begin with the Word of God.

DWELL IN TRUTH YOU CAN KNOW.

- To dwell in truth is to make your home there. That means God's truth dominates your thoughts and attitudes, governs your life, and satisfies your heart.

- God gives us plenty of truth in the Bible that we can know and trust. Those 66 books, 1189 chapters, are trustworthy. They (the Scriptures) can be investigated to show that the biblical records are trustworthy.

- God wants us to know the truth He has revealed to us, to make our home in that truth. Each passage we read or study has plenty of truth that we can know with certainty and allow to govern our lives.

HUMBLY ACCEPT WHAT YOU DON'T KNOW OR UNDERSTAND.

- Some things we read in the Bible we don't understand now but might in the future. There is much we can know now. But there are things we'll never know or understand. *Deuteronomy 29:29*

- We can do our best to try to understand what is written. When you run across something that you can't seem to understand from a Bible passage, make the choice to humbly accept what you don't know or understand and be satisfied with it.

DISCERN ALL TEACHING THROUGH THE COMPLETE REVELATION OF GOD'S WORD.

1. Evaluate what you read and hear by comparing it with the whole Bible.

- We can't take pieces of the Bible, like a verse or group of verses, and build our thinking on that. And we shouldn't let experiences and feelings become our measures of truth. There's junk out there about God so it's important to really get to know the God of the Bible and what He says to us. All false teachers throughout the centuries have taken advantage of people who were not dwelling in the truth revealed in the whole Bible.

- Even the best teachers are not infallible. Always check what you read and hear with what the Word of God says.

2. Avoid the "look-imagine-see dragon" when viewing any verse.

The "look-imagine-see dragon" shows up this way: someone *looks* at a verse or passage, *imagines* what they want it to say, then in their mind *sees* what they have imagined through twisting word meanings and interpretations. Once it starts, it's like a fiery dragon burning truth in its path. Cultural influence on Bible study feeds this dragon.

- Tame the "look-imagine-see dragon" by considering the Bible as sufficient on its own, not needing to be "improved" by us.

- Tame the "look-imagine-see dragon" by basing your faith on what **is** in God's Word, not something you've just heard about it and not something you're imagining to be there.

- Tame the "look-imagine-see dragon" by **following the inductive process for Bible Study.** That's the process we use in all of our *Joyful Walk Bible Studies.*

  ✓ We start off every day's study with asking for the Lord to teach us. The Holy Spirit inside will give us understanding as we read and study.
  ✓ Then, we answer the question, "What does it say?" We have you look directly at the text—what it actually says, not what you have heard it say, or what someone else says about it. Good Bible study reads a verse in the context of the passage where it is found—the paragraph, the chapter, and the book. Each verse is usually part of a continual thought.
  ✓ The next question to ask in the process is this, "What does it mean?" That is not what it means to you or to your neighbor or to your Facebook friend. But what did it mean at the time it was written? You can examine the original words to learn what the writer meant and what the audience likely understood. You can look at other verses with similar content to let the Bible interpret itself. Then, you can understand what it means for you today.
  ✓ Once you know what the Bible says and what it means (truth over opinion), then you are ready for application, which is learning how to live this out in your life.

  The Bible is the greatest of all books; to study it is the noblest of all pursuits; to understand it, the highest of all goals. (Charles Ryrie)

Let Jesus satisfy your heart with His perspective on life in the present and in the future. Then, live securely in Him during this time of waiting.

5: Perspective on Faithful Endurance

1 Thessalonians 3:1-13

DAY ONE STUDY—GET THE BIG PICTURE

Ask the Lord Jesus to teach you through His Word.

What does the Bible say?

Read the Bible passage below (NIV) including verses from the last lesson. Use your own method (colored pencils, lines, shapes) to mark 1) anything that grabs your attention, 2) words you want to understand, and 3) topics you have seen before in this letter. Draw arrows between thoughts that connect.

2 *[17] But, brothers and sisters, when we were orphaned by being separated from you for a short time (in person, not in thought), out of our intense longing we made every effort to see you. [18] For we wanted to come to you—certainly I, Paul, did, again and again—but Satan blocked our way. [19] For what is our hope, our joy, or the crown in which we will glory in the presence of our Lord Jesus when he comes? Is it not you? [20] Indeed, you are our glory and joy.*

3 *[1] So when we could stand it no longer, we thought it best to be left by ourselves in Athens. [2] We sent Timothy, who is our brother and co-worker in God's service in spreading the gospel of Christ, to strengthen and encourage you in your faith, [3] so that no one would be unsettled by these trials. For you know quite well that we are destined for them. [4] In fact, when we were with you, we kept telling you that we would be persecuted. And it turned out that way, as you well know. [5] For this reason, when I could stand it no longer, I sent to find out about your faith. I was afraid that in some way the tempter had tempted you and that our labors might have been in vain.*

[6] But Timothy has just now come to us from you and has brought good news about your faith and love. He has told us that you always have pleasant memories of us and that you long to see us, just as we also long to see you. [7] Therefore, brothers and sisters, in all our distress and persecution we were encouraged about you because of your faith. [8] For now we really live, since you are standing firm in the Lord.

[9] How can we thank God enough for you in return for all the joy we have in the presence of our God because of you? [10] Night and day we pray most earnestly that we may see you again and supply what is lacking in your faith.

[11] Now may our God and Father himself and our Lord Jesus clear the way for us to come to you. [12] May the Lord make your love increase and overflow for each other and for everyone else, just as ours does for you. [13] May he strengthen your hearts so that you will be blameless and holy in the presence of our God and Father when our Lord Jesus comes with all his holy ones.

1. What grabbed your attention from 3:1-13?

2. What verses or specific words do you want to understand better?

3. What words or phrases are repeated in this passage? Give verses.

4. What topics (if any) in this passage have we studied in previous lessons?

5. *Gain perspective:* From this lesson's passage (3:1-13), choose one verse to dwell upon all week long. Write it in the space below. Ask God to teach you through this verse.

Respond to the Lord about what you learned today.

Day Two Study

Read 1 Thessalonians 3:1-13. Ask the Lord Jesus to teach you through His Word.

What does the Bible say?

Today, we will focus on vv. 1-8.

6. Answer the following questions to better follow the narrative given.

   What decision did Paul make (v. 1)?

   Whom did he send and why (vv. 2-3)?

   What did Paul know would happen (v. 4)?

   What problem did Paul recognize (v. 5)?

   What news did Timothy bring back from Thessalonica (v. 6)?

   How did this news affect Paul (vv. 7-8)?

7. *Deeper Discoveries (optional):* Timothy was likely 18 or so when he joined Paul's second missionary journey. Read Acts 16:1-3; 2 Timothy 1:2-5; 3:14-15; and Philippians 2:19-22. What do you learn about Timothy?

What does it mean?

8. Paul refers to "trials" in v. 3. The Greek word translated as "trials" means "pressing together, pressure" and refers to any trouble that causes anguish and distress, whether from the burdens of life or persecution. Trials in this context, though, refers to persecution from hostile fellow citizens (1 Thessalonians 1:6; 2:14). The word *destined* means "certain to meet, according to a plan." Read the following verses to explain what Paul meant when he said that believers are *destined* for that kind of trial.

   • John 15:18-21—

- Philippians 1:29-30—

- 2 Timothy 3:12—

9. Read 2 Corinthians 1:8-9; 4:16-17. How should a Christ-follower think when it comes to such trials?

> **Dependent Living:** Beware of a false teaching that says, "God doesn't give you more than you can handle." Of course, He does! Paul testified to that in 2 Corinthians 1:8. After all those years of serving God, if God wanted Paul to rely on Him rather than on his own figuring out, you can be confident that God wants the same for you. God gives all of us more than we can handle on our own in order to drive us to Him so that we will depend on Him more than on ourselves.

10. The last lesson focused on the benefits of suffering. This lesson will focus on our response to suffering. Read Matthew 5:43-48 and Romans 12:14, 17-21. How should a Christ-follower respond to harsh treatment from others?

11. Regardless of the kind of trial causing anguish, how should one Christ-follower encourage another who is undergoing such distress? Consider all that you've learned so far.

12. Because of the persecution, Paul's concern (v. 5) is the Thessalonian believers might have been tempted to do what? Consider their background.

Dependent Living: Often new believers, and even older believers, interpret difficulty as a sign that God is mad at them or that they have done something wrong. That is the pagan view of trouble not the biblical view of trouble. God allows troubles in our lives to teach us faithful endurance as we rely on Him.

13. Temptation is not sin, but during trials, believers might be tempted to sin through giving up, taking revenge, or compromise. What does the Lord promise to us regarding temptation?

- 1 Corinthians 10:12-13—

- Hebrews 4:14-16—

Scriptural Insight: The tempter (1 Thessalonians 3:5) is Satan (Matthew 4:1-3). Although God allows him freedom to tempt believers, remember that he has already been defeated on the cross (Colossians 2:15), and Christians need not be overwhelmed by him as they learn to rely on God more and more in their lives.

14. ***Deeper Discoveries (optional):*** Go to gotquestions.org and type in the question, "Who is Satan?" Read the information and scriptures given in the answer. What do you learn?

15. Paul had a healthy fear (concern) for the Thessalonians (v. 5). Fear is a normal human emotion designed by God to alert us to danger so that we will take action against it. Paul sent Timothy back to them (v. 2). What news did Timothy bring back to Paul (vv. 6-8)?

Think About It: One of the meanings of the Greek word translated "really live" in v. 8 is "to breathe." As a result of that action, Paul basically said he could "breathe again." We often use that phrase today, "able to breathe again," when we no longer need to be afraid or worried about someone or something. Consider how parents feel when they send their kids off to college then hear that they are thriving there rather than sinking. Or consider how you feel when someone you love travels far away and you finally hear from them that they are safe. That's what Paul was experiencing.

What application will you make to gain a biblical perspective?

16. As a member of the Body of Christ, you should hurt when another part of the Body is hurting (1 Corinthians 12:25-27). You may not be undergoing persecution or suffering at the moment, but you likely know someone who is. Read 2 Corinthians 1:3-5, 11 and Ephesians 6:18. What can you do to share in the pain of persecution or other suffering and give comfort where needed? Consider also what Paul did in this lesson.

Respond to the Lord about what you learned today.

DAY THREE STUDY

Read 1 Thessalonians 3:1-13. Ask the Lord Jesus to teach you through His Word.

What does it mean?

Today, we will focus on vv. 9-13.

17. After Paul received the good news about the Thessalonians (vv. 6-8) …

- What was his response to God (v. 9)?

- Based on what you've learned so far in 1 Thessalonians, why did he feel that way?

18. For what was he frequently praying for the Thessalonians (v. 10)?

19. Paul used the word "faith" 5 times in this chapter. Faith needs to be fed with truth so believers will know how to live. Considering how new to the faith those Thessalonian Christians were, what could Paul have meant by the phrase, "supply what is lacking in your faith" (v. 10)? See also 1 Thessalonians 2:12 and 4:1.

Think About It: If he couldn't come in person, he could send Timothy to teach, and he could write. Chapters 4 and 5 in this letter teach truths to help them live to please God.

20. It is evident from Paul's writings that a very large part of his private life was occupied in prayer and thanksgiving. And prayer was his default response to whatever life threw at him. In 1 Thessalonians 2:17-18 and 3:10-11, Paul expressed his longing (literally "passionate, intense longing") to be with the new church again.

- What did Paul ask God to do (v. 11)?

- How do we know Paul was willing to wait for the Lord's timing?

21. In vv. 12-13, Paul prayed a beautiful, heartfelt prayer for the new church at Thessalonica. Considering their current life experiences, why would their love need to "increase and overflow" for not only fellow church members but others as well?

Think About It: This kind of love was described by the late author, Francis Schaeffer, as "the mark of the Christian." God is the source of this kind of love.

22. ***Deeper Discoveries (optional):*** We humans need to learn how to live a life of love (Ephesians 5:1-2) God's way. What would that look like in our thoughts and behavior toward others? Read 1 Corinthians 13:4-7 and Colossians 3:5-17 to answer that question.

23. Paul also prayed that God would strengthen their hearts so they would be blameless and holy (v. 13). Read the "Scriptural Insight" then answer the question below it.

Scriptural Insight: To be holy means to be set apart from sin and to God. The Bible uses the term "sanctified" to describe this in 1 Thessalonians 4:3. By faith in Jesus Christ, God declares us holy in His sight. We are clothed with Christ (Galatians 3:27). When God looks on you and me, He sees Jesus and His righteousness, not all of our faults. His love chooses to do that for us. You have been set apart as God's special, beloved possession for His exclusive use. You are also "being made holy" in your thoughts, words, and actions by the work of the Holy Spirit. This is ongoing from the moment of salvation until the Lord comes or you die, when your "being made holy" is complete.

We make choices that reflect our desire to set ourselves apart from sin and to God's purposes for us. Read 2 Corinthians 7:1 and Titus 2:11-12. What do you learn about choices you can make to strengthen your heart so you will be blameless and holy?

24. We are to live now with the perspective of what will happen in our future. Jesus is coming with whom (v. 13)? See also 1 Thessalonians 4:14, 16.

25. Read Hebrews 12:1-3. The holy ones coming with Jesus are the witnesses. They are believers in God who lived before us and stayed faithful in spite of trials. Based on Hebrews 12:1, what are we encouraged to do now during the waiting?

Jesus is our example of how to live through suffering. He is also the one who enables us to stay faithful to Him through suffering (1 Thessalonians 5:24).

What application will you make to gain a biblical perspective?

26. *About loving others during suffering:* What has God taught you about growing in your love for others, even during trials? What do you still need to learn? Ask Him for that today using the prayer in 1 Thessalonians 3:12.

27. *About pursuing holiness:* What has God taught you about separating yourself from sin and wickedness, even during trials? What do you still need to learn? Ask Him for that today using the prayer in 1 Thessalonians 3:13.

28. *About waiting for God with patient endurance:*

- When you desperately want something that seems out of your reach, what is your typical reaction? Do you ever allow God to "clear the way" for you in His own perfect timing?

- Read Psalm 40:1-3. Consider anything you have patiently endured. What did you learn through that? With whom have you shared your "new song" of God's faithfulness in your life?

Pray 1 Thessalonians 3:12-13 for yourself and others.

Recommended: Listen to the podcast "Gain the Biblical Perspective on Suffering" after doing this lesson to reinforce what you have learned. Use the listener guide on the next page.

Gain the Biblical Perspective on Suffering

Through the past 2000 years, many Christians facing persecution have chosen to stay faithful to Jesus no matter the cost. But staying faithful no matter the cost requires endurance.

STAYING FAITHFUL REQUIRES ENDURANCE.

For our light and momentary troubles are achieving for us an eternal glory that outweighs them all. (2 Corinthians 4:17)

- Jesus said to His followers that we will have trouble in this world. All of us. Some troubles like illness and natural disasters come from living in this fallen world and are common to everyone. Other troubles like persecution and rejection are related to being a child of God living in an unbelieving world. Then there are those we inflict upon ourselves because of sin still present within us—our own bad choices—or troubles that others inflict upon us because of their bad choices. Either way, we get stuck with the results.

- Any kind of suffering is painful. We don't need to pretend that it isn't painful. We can grieve over the losses or what is being denied to us that we desire. Jesus understands the pain we experience.

- Jesus wants to help us not only survive a lifetime of ups and downs but also to thrive as we live through them. For that, we need **endurance**, something that Jesus had and that the Bible says is good for us. Endurance is only learned when there is a challenge to our comfort. Biblical endurance encompasses the necessity of perseverance. *2 Thessalonians 1:4*

By definition, perseverance is holding to a course of action, a belief, or a purpose without giving way.

Truth #1: Endurance is good for us.

- "Endurance" or "perseverance" in the Bible is a strong word that means holding up a load with staying power and stick-to-it-iveness. Endurance carries the idea of whole life experience.

- Biblical endurance is the quality that enables a person to stand on his or her feet when facing a storm head on. Endurance is good for us. It teaches us "staying power" for a long-term burden.

Truth #2: Endurance makes us stronger.

- Bible study alone won't develop endurance. Just like load-bearing exercise makes your bones stronger, troubles that challenge your faith do that, too. Biblical endurance through suffering makes us stronger.

Truth #3: Endurance is necessary to grow up into maturity.

- In the process of human development, painful experiences are necessary for developing into a fully functioning, responsible adult. When we overprotect children from going through troubles, they don't develop endurance and maturity.

- Good character is enhanced through tough times as you endure and overcome them. God uses suffering to humble and test you in order to know what is in your heart. *Romans 5:3-5; Deuteronomy 8:2*

- God strengthened the Thessalonians so that they were able to stand firm in the Lord in spite of the severe suffering. God's goal for us is to be mature and complete.

Truth #4: Endurance is necessary to reject corrupting influences.

- Bad company corrupts good character. *1 Corinthians 15:33*

- Recognize corrupting influences through certain characteristics. *2 Corinthians 11:19-20*
    - ✓ They enslave you to make you do what they want by their own rules.
    - ✓ They exploit you by taking your things and making money or gain off of you.
    - ✓ They take advantage of you, knowing your weakness and how to gain power over you.
    - ✓ They push themselves forward, lording over you, even bullying you.
    - ✓ They slap you in the face, meaning they are cruel, mean, and abusive.
    - ✓ They are idle, ready to join any anti-authoritarian mob because they have no noble goals.

- When you encounter people with those characteristics, the Bible says to flee from them. You can live without them. You don't have to put up with them.

Truth #5: Endurance teaches us to depend on God more than on ourselves.

- The popular saying, "God doesn't give you more than you can handle" is a false teaching. God gives us more than we can handle on our own. *2 Corinthians 1:8-9*

- Going through troubles is God's will for us (Deuteronomy 8:2). He allows things in our lives to challenge us. It is not so we don't need Him any longer but that we would rely on Him more. God gives everyone more than we can handle on our own in order to drive us to Him. When we do so, we see that He is worthy of our trust.

    I waited patiently for the Lord; he turned to me and heard my cry. He lifted me out of the slimy pit, out of the mud and mire; he set my feet on a rock and gave me a firm place to stand. He put a new song in my mouth, a hymn of praise to our God. Many will see and fear the Lord and put their trust in him. (Psalm 40:1-3)

Let Jesus satisfy your heart with His perspective on life in the present and in the future. Then, live securely in Him during this time of waiting.

6: Perspective on Sex and Love

1 Thessalonians 4:1-12

DAY ONE STUDY—GET THE BIG PICTURE

Ask the Lord Jesus to teach you through His Word.

What does the Bible say?

Read the Bible passage below (NIV) including verses from the last lesson. Use your own method (colored pencils, lines, shapes) to mark 1) anything that grabs your attention, 2) words you want to understand, and 3) topics you have seen before in this letter. Draw arrows between thoughts that connect.

3 *[12] May the Lord make your love increase and overflow for each other and for everyone else, just as ours does for you. [13] May he strengthen your hearts so that you will be blameless and holy in the presence of our God and Father when our Lord Jesus comes with all his holy ones.*

4 *[1] As for other matters, brothers and sisters, we instructed you how to live in order to please God, as in fact you are living. Now we ask you and urge you in the Lord Jesus to do this more and more. [2] For you know what instructions we gave you by the authority of the Lord Jesus.*

[3] It is God's will that you should be sanctified: that you should avoid sexual immorality; [4] that each of you should learn to control your own body in a way that is holy and honorable, [5] not in passionate lust like the pagans, who do not know God; [6] and that in this matter no one should wrong or take advantage of a brother or sister. The Lord will punish all those who commit such sins, as we told you and warned you before. [7] For God did not call us to be impure, but to live a holy life. [8] Therefore, anyone who rejects this instruction does not reject a human being but God, the very God who gives you his Holy Spirit.

[9] Now about your love for one another we do not need to write to you, for you yourselves have been taught by God to love each other. [10] And in fact, you do love all of God's family throughout Macedonia. Yet we urge you, brothers and sisters, to do so more and more, [11] and to make it your ambition to lead a quiet life: You should mind your own business and work with your hands, just as we told you, [12] so that your daily life may win the respect of outsiders and so that you will not be dependent on anybody.

1. What grabbed your attention from 4:1-12?

2. What verses or specific words do you want to understand better?

3. What words or phrases are repeated in this passage? Give verses.

4. What topics (if any) in this passage have we studied in previous lessons?

5. *Gain perspective:* From this lesson's passage (4:1-12), choose one verse to dwell upon all week long. Write it in the space below. Ask God to teach you through this verse.

Respond to the Lord about what you learned today.

DAY TWO STUDY

Read 1 Thessalonians 4:1-12. Ask the Lord Jesus to teach you through His Word.

What does it mean?

Today, we will focus on vv. 1-8.

6. According to v. 1, what should determine the life choices of every believer? See also 1 Thessalonians 2:4; Colossians 1:10; and John 8:29. Remember our "Audience of One" (Lesson 3).

> **Think About It:** The Christian life is not a set of rules to be obeyed or a list of prohibitions to avoid; it is the outworking of a loving desire to **please God** who chose us. (*The Bible Knowledge Commentary New Testament,* p. 700)

Such a decision influences every part of life, especially those areas where the culture teaches otherwise, such as sexual behavior. The Mosaic Law was very clear on God's design of sex for marriage between a man and a woman (Genesis 2:24-25) and His expectation of His people to avoid sexual immorality (Leviticus chapter 18). The Jews were not immune to sexual immorality, and Jesus hit them hard on the subject (see Matthew 5:27-28; John 8:2-11). But the Gentile culture was far worse. That is why sexual immorality was included in the "4 things to avoid" letter sent to Gentile Christians in Acts 15:19-20.

> **Historical Insight:** The Greeks practiced sexual immorality commonly, and even incorporated it into their religious practices. Pagan religion did not demand sexual purity of its devotees, the gods and goddesses being grossly immoral. Priestesses were in the temples for the service of the men who came. Greek men were known to keep prostitutes and mistresses. So long as a man supported his wife and family, there was no shame whatsoever in extra-marital relationships. (*Dr. Constable's Notes on 1 Thessalonians 2020 Edition,* p. 44)

7. As believers, we sometimes fret because we can't figure out God's will on some matter in our lives. Yet, He has given us specific direction about a great many things. What is declared with certainty to be God's will for all believers in v. 3? See also v. 7.

Remember that being sanctified (holiness) means to be **set apart** from sin and to God's purposes in your life. Because of our faith in Christ, God declares us to be holy in status. The indwelling Holy Spirit goes to work in us to make us holy in our thoughts and behavior so that we are like Jesus Christ (1 Thessalonians 3:13; 2 Corinthians 3:18; Romans 8:29). We make choices that reflect our desire to set ourselves apart from sin and to God's purposes for us. Being sanctified also involves abstinence (self-denial) of behavior that is outside the prescribed will of God.

8. Paul wrote to believers who had already been declared holy by their position in Christ. His teaching is now referring to their present conduct.

   - Read 1 Corinthians 6:13-20 and Ephesians 5:1-4. Why should believers be "set apart for the Lord" regarding sex?

   - Would you agree that holiness and sexual immorality are mutually exclusive? Why or why not? See Romans 8:5-8.

9. Look at 1 Thessalonians 4:4-5. The Greek word translated "control" or "possess" in verse 4 carried the idea of gaining mastery over something. And Paul commonly used the word for "vessel" in his writings to describe one's own body (as "jars of clay" in 2 Corinthians 4:7).

   - What does it mean to control your own body in a way that is holy and honorable? Holy and honorable to whom?

   - Contrast that with the description in verse 5.

      Focus on the Meaning: God's plan for a Christian includes purifying her life. Sexual immorality frustrates the purpose of God's call.... **A holy life demonstrates God's supernatural power at work overcoming what is natural,** and it glorifies God. (*The Bible Knowledge Commentary New Testament*, p. 702)

10. ***Deeper Discoveries (optional):*** Read Genesis 2:24-25; 1 Corinthians 7:1-5; and Hebrews 13:4. Concerning God's design of sex, does God say what He wants? Add other verses that support this.

Scriptural Insight: Physical love in marriage, symbolically uniting two personalities by the outward act of sexual intercourse, is beautiful in the eyes of God. And it is holy...The *Song of Solomon* is a very romantic book in which God communicates to us His delight in the wonderful relationship between a man and woman in marriage...God made us sexual beings. Marriage has been provided to satisfy such needs, and every scriptural prohibition has to do with sexual activity outside marriage. Don't let anyone tell you the Bible prohibits sex or represses your sexuality. (Vickie Kraft, *Influential Woman*, pp. 64-70)

11. In verse 6, Paul used two words to describe actions that hurt others. The words translated "wrong" and "take advantage" both mean to take more than you should, to overreach, to step over the limits to gain an advantage over.

   • What do you think Paul means by saying not to wrong or take advantage of a brother or sister in the area of sexual behavior? Consider examples of this in life.

   • Why should you take this admonition seriously? What does God promise to do about it whenever you wrong or take advantage of another person in the area of sexual behavior?

   Focus on the Meaning: Sexual immorality wrongs the partner by involving him or her in behavior contrary to God's will and therefore under His judgment...The initiation of the act takes advantage of the other person by fanning the fire of passion until self-control is lost. This is not referring to rape, incest, or sexual molestation. Those are acts of violence perpetrated on an innocent person. God acting as Avenger would certainly apply in those situations as well. (*The Bible Knowledge Commentary New Testament*, pp. 701-702)

12. As you have seen from today's passage, God takes a position on sex.

   • When you reject biblical teaching about sexual behavior, what are you really doing (v. 8)? Why is this not a wise thing to do?

   • Based on this study of 1 Thessalonians, what can you say to someone, especially a Christian, who says they don't accept biblical standards because they don't apply today?

In the first century, moral standards were generally low, and chastity was regarded as an unreasonable restriction. Sound familiar? According to recent surveys, the morality of Christians is not much different from that of non-Christians in the area of sex. For many of us, holding to God's standard of sexual morality may mean that we honor His word more than our own opinions. How easy is that for you?

> **Scriptural Insight:** The indwelling Holy Spirit has power enough to enable any Christian to learn how to control his own body, even in a pagan immoral climate. The exhortation is to avoid sexual immorality; the enablement comes from the Holy Spirit. (*The Bible Knowledge Commentary New Testament,* pp. 702)

What application will you make to gain a biblical perspective?

13. *If someone has wronged you or taken advantage of you in the past:* Read Ephesians 4:30-32 and Romans 12:17-19. As a forgiven believer in Jesus Christ, what should you do? Consider also what you learned in today's lesson.

14. *If you are presently caught in sexual immorality:* All sin (past, present, and future) is forgiven the moment anyone trusts in Christ. Yet, the sin nature remains in our bodies as long as we live on this earth. Because we are not perfected, we will continue to sin both unintentionally and intentionally. Our sins are forgiven, but our God knows that continuing sinful behavior is not good for us and does not please Him. If you are in a sexually immoral relationship or behavior pattern, and want to please God with your life, follow this biblical process to deal with that recognized sin:

> **Step One: View yourself rightly.** Your identity is not that immoral sin. You are in Christ, a child of God, who sometimes sins against God in that way.

> **Step Two: Recognize (confess) the truth regarding your sin.** To confess biblically means to agree with God about what you and He both know to be true. Confession is not a formula, a process, or dependent on a mediator. Regarding sin in your life, it is not just saying, "I'm sorry." It is saying, "I agree with you, God. I blew it!" You see your sin as something awful! Considering sexual immorality, the Spirit has convicted you from this lesson that sexual immorality in any form is not pleasing to God. You are instructed to flee or avoid immorality. You recognize this sin in your life. You agree with God that your immoral sexual behavior is seeking love and acceptance from the wrong source. It doesn't fit someone who knows God. That is confession.

> **Step Three: Confession is incomplete without repentance.** Repentance means to change your mind about that sin, to turn away from it, to mourn its ugliness, resulting in changing your actions. Paul says in 2 Corinthians 7:9-11 that godly sorrow brings repentance. It's saying, "I recognize what I am doing is wrong. This fills me with sorrow because it hurts You, God. Please help me to live differently." And that is how

our lives get transformed. If you want to live in order to please God, then you know that God wants you to avoid sexual immorality. So you can pray, "Lord Jesus, please have your Spirit nudge me when I am not holy and honorable with my body. Help me to say no to temptation and to give up any relationship and behavior that is not honorable to you. By faith, Lord, I want you to do that in my life." That is repentance. Repentance isn't repentance until you change something. You can confess "until the cows come home" (daily, habitually) and never change anything. Jesus called for people to "repent" not just "confess."

Step Four: Repentance leads to dependence. Depend on the living Christ inside you for that change to take place, whatever it is. Our Lord Jesus Christ is not interested in our compliance or outward conformity as much as He desires our obedience from the heart. Memorize 1 Thessalonians 4:3-7 and any other scriptures that deal with staying pure and not rejecting God's instructions. Be sensitive to the Spirit's nudging when you are tempted to do otherwise. And choose to desire a life that pleases God. It's right to say, "Lord Jesus, I can't do this on my own. I trust you to do this in me and through me." Then, watch what He does!

15. *Deeper Discoveries (optional):* Masturbation is a hot topic in our modern culture with many views, even among Christians. Since the Bible doesn't mention this self-stimulation specifically, you must use what the Bible does say about sex and its purpose to derive a biblical perspective on this subject. God designed sex for marriage. Masturbation within the marriage relationship where the husband and wife are thinking about each other would still fit within God's purpose. When that is accompanied by fantasy, pornography, or adulterous thoughts, one crosses the line into immorality. For a single person, any kind of sexual activity outside of marriage is against God's purpose for sex. Here are two resources that give thoughtful insight for you: "Does the Bible say that masturbation is sin?" on Bible.org. and "Questions and Concerns about Masturbation" on focusonthefamily.com.

Respond to the Lord about what you learned today.

DAY THREE STUDY

Read 1 Thessalonians 4:1-12. Ask the Lord Jesus to teach you through His Word.

What does it mean?

Today, we will focus on vv. 9-12.

> **From the Greek:** The phrase translated "love for each other (NIV)" or "brotherly love (ESV)" translates *philadelphia*, a Greek word that outside the New Testament almost without exception denoted the mutual love of children of the same father. In the New Testament, it always means love of fellow believers in Christ, all of whom have the same heavenly Father. (*The NIV Study Bible*, p. 1824)

16. In verses 9-10, Paul referred again to the love the Thessalonians had for each other (1 Thessalonians 1:3; 3:12). He said that they had been taught by God to love each other.

    • Read John 13:1, 15, 34-35. How does Jesus teach us about love?

    • Read 1 John 4:7-12. How does God teach us about love?

17. How does following God's instructions about sex in 1 Thessalonians 4:1-8 fit with loving one another more and more (vv. 9-10)?

18. After urging them to love one another more and more,

    • What three things should they also do (v. 11)?

    • Why (v. 12)?

Let's examine verse 11 more closely, phrase by phrase, and see how these three aspects of behavior demonstrate love for others.

19. *Make it your ambition to lead a quiet life:*

- The word translated "quiet" means quiet in the sense of restfulness and peacefulness. It refers to being undisturbed and settled, not frantic and restless. It is not saying you must lead a life of silence with no talking or exuberance. What could "to lead a quiet life" mean? See also 1 Timothy 2:1-4 and consider what the Thessalonians were experiencing.

- "Make it your ambition" means to strive earnestly, make it your aim or goal. Why would aiming to lead "a quiet life" be a good thing for yourself as well as for others?

20. *Mind your own business:*

- "To mind your own business" means "to do or manage that which pertains to you." Contrast what it means to mind or attend to your own business with the opposite of doing that. See also 2 Thessalonians 3:11.

- How would minding your own business demonstrate brotherly love for other believers?

21. *Work with your hands:*

> **Historical Insight:** The Greeks deplored manual labor and relegated it to slaves as much as possible. But the Jews held it in esteem; every Jewish boy was taught a trade regardless of his family's wealth. Work itself is a blessing, and working with one's hands should never be despised by Christians." (*The Bible Knowledge Commentary New Testament,* p. 703)

The phrase "work with your hands" doesn't mean just using your hands as in manual labor. It refers to any work that you do by your own efforts to support yourself.

- Read 1 Thessalonians 2:6-9 and 2 Thessalonians 3:7-10. How had Paul set the example for them and why?

- How would doing this demonstrate love for and benefit other believers? See also Ephesians 4:28.

Dependent Living: Notice that Paul's intent was not to change the society. He encouraged Christians to rely on God to change their hearts and behavior to be like Christ. In that way, they would become the best citizens they could be and benefit their society in more ways than they could ever do on their own.

What application will you make to gain a biblical perspective?

22. *About leading a "quiet life":* If your life is hectic, what actions should you take to make it less hectic and disruptive to those around you? Do you influence your family members, neighbors, or co-workers *away* from living a "quiet life?" Talk to God about this and ask Him to work in your heart first. Then, ask Him to direct you towards leading a quiet life.

23. *About minding your own business:* Are you tempted to meddle in other people's lives? If so, do you recognize this as a distraction from your own walk with God as well as theirs? Ask Jesus to help you not try to "fix" people or situations but to direct them to the Lord first.

24. *About working:* How do you view your work? Is it only a means to a paycheck? Or do you consider your work as a way to live out your faith in the view of your co-workers? Read Colossians 3:23-24. What do you learn about this?

Respond to the Lord about what you learned today.

Recommended: Listen to the podcast "Gain the Biblical Perspective on Sex and the Flesh" after doing this lesson to reinforce what you have learned. Use the listener guide on the next page.

Gain the Biblical Perspective on Sex and the Flesh

WHAT IS THE FLESH?

The flesh is the personality of a human controlled by sin and directed to selfish pursuits rather than the service of God. (Dr. Charles Ryrie)

- God created this marvelous human body for us. The body is not evil in itself. But sin which indwells our humanity—that is the enemy. Since the time of Adam, every human has been born with a sinful nature.

- We don't know what it is, but we know how the flesh works. It sends messages to the mind that are in conflict with the Spirit. The work of the flesh is obvious and ugly. *Mark 7; Galatians 5*

WHY DOES THE FLESH ASSAULT US?

- When we trust in Christ as our Savior, we get forgiveness for our sin, and we get new life as the Holy Spirit comes to live inside our once-dead spirits to make us spiritually alive.

- Our human spirit communicates with the Holy Spirit. We have direct access to God who is our Father. We are made into a new creation—spiritually.

- We now possess the life of the new creation through the Holy Spirit in us while still living in bodies of the old, fallen creation in a fallen, evil world. At the moment of salvation, we are born again of the Spirit. Our bodies are **not** born again. And our souls—that is, the mind, emotions, and will—are **not** instantly transformed.

WE NEED TO KNOW THIS ENEMY TO HAVE VICTORY OVER IT.

The New Testament teaches us some truths about the flesh we must know to have victory over it.

- ✓ **Truth #1:** The desires of the flesh won't go away. You choose to gratify them or not.
- ✓ **Truth #2:** The flesh doesn't improve over time. It does not become "godly" over time.
- ✓ **Truth #3:** The flesh won't leave us alone to be spiritual. *Romans 6*
- ✓ **Truth #4:** The flesh wants control. There will be continual conflict. *Romans 7*
- ✓ **Truth #5:** The flesh doesn't become less able to be tempted over time.
- ✓ **Truth #6:** The flesh uses a consistent pattern: Sending a thought to your mind leading to familiarity with that thought, leading to a loss of repugnance, and, eventually, leading to curiosity and a desire to experiment with an activity. Having tried the activity, the flesh learns to like it, and even grow dependent, on any sensual stimulus.

THE CULTURE FEEDS THE FLESH, ESPECIALLY REGARDING SEX.

See to it that no one takes you captive through hollow and deceptive philosophy, which depends on human tradition and the elemental spiritual forces of this world rather than on Christ. (Colossians 2:8)

- Whenever human ideas are separated from Christ and the Bible, they are hollow and deceptive philosophies. But even more than that, they are under the influence of Satan and his demons. *Ephesians 2*

- Paul says stay away from any system of thought that depends on and gives credit to human thought and tradition more than to Jesus Christ. When considering anyone's philosophy, the qualifying test is this: Where does Jesus fit into their thinking? If their thinking says he is just a way to know God or just a good teacher, and we accept that thinking, then we trade the core and eternal truth of Christ for lies. If their thinking is He is just the way to get saved and go to heaven when we die, but doesn't care about what you do now, then you have turned Him into a ticket for a destination and devalued Him as Lord. Either way, we allow ourselves to be "taken captive" by the culture.

WHAT MAKES US SUSCEPTIBLE TO THIS CULTURAL CAPTIVITY?

Cultural captivity looks to the culture rather than to Christ and the Bible as truth and a primary guide for living. Cultural captivity is usually caused by 3 things: Putting our trust in something other than the person or promises of Christ, misunderstanding the truths by which Christ has called us to live, or a combination of both. (Probe Ministries)

- The culture's teachings lead Christians to think the culture will satisfy your heart needs more than Christ. So you become more likely to side with your culture rather than with Christ or the Bible, even on those religious practices or cultural issues clearly addressed in the Bible.

VICTORY COMES THROUGH DEPENDENCE ON THE SPIRIT OF GOD TO OVERCOME THE DESIRES OF THE FLESH.

- "Living by the Spirit" or "walking by the Spirit" is dependence on the Spirit of God to empower you to say no to the flesh and say yes to obedience to God. The blood of Jesus paid your freedom price so you no longer have to obey the flesh. The Bible calls that redemption. You have a new master with greater power than the flesh living inside of you now—the Spirit of God Himself. He can give you freedom from any entrapping sin. *Titus 2:11-14; Galatians 5:16*

- We never outgrow our need to depend 100% upon Jesus Christ. Recognizing this should lead us to have compassion on one another and to not take risks with sinful behavior!

- Seek to depend on Christ more in your life than on yourself. It's okay to say, "Lord, I can't do this on my own. But you can do this in me and through me." Then, watch what he does!

The more we choose God's truth and God's way, the easier it becomes to resist the lies of the enemy and turn away from the temptations of the flesh. (Teasi Cannon, *Mama Bear Apologetics,* p. 91)

Let Jesus satisfy your heart with His perspective on life in the present and in the future. Then, live securely in Him during this time of waiting.

7: Perspective on Death and Beyond

1 Thessalonians 4:13-18

DAY ONE STUDY—GET THE BIG PICTURE

Ask the Lord Jesus to teach you through His Word.

Trying to understand prophecy about the future is like having a bunch of puzzle pieces that look similar but without the picture on the box top to tell you how to arrange them. All we know for sure are the border pieces. We can put the 4 sides of the puzzle together. Those are events we know will definitely happen, but we don't know when or how the rest of the pieces fit inside the border.

Paul described one such event in 1 Thessalonians chapter 4. This is Christ appearing as Savior to gather all believers, dead and alive, together with Him in the clouds. A second event is the Great Tribulation during which God's wrath against sin is directed toward earth. That is introduced in 1 Thessalonians chapter 5. Another event is the revealing of the Antichrist, described as the man of lawlessness in 2 Thessalonians chapter 2. The fourth event is Christ coming in judgment on unbelievers and setting up His kingdom on earth. That's described in 2 Thessalonians chapter 1. Those are the 4 sides to our puzzle.

What does the Bible say?

Read the Bible passage below (NIV) including verses from the last lesson. Use your own method (colored pencils, lines, shapes) to mark 1) anything that grabs your attention, 2) words you want to understand, and 3) topics you have seen before in this letter. Draw arrows between thoughts that connect.

4 *9 Now about your love for one another we do not need to write to you, for you yourselves have been taught by God to love each other. 10 And in fact, you do love all of God's family throughout Macedonia. Yet we urge you, brothers and sisters, to do so more and more, 11 and to make it your ambition to lead a quiet life: You should mind your own business and work with your hands, just as we told you, 12 so that your daily life may win the respect of outsiders and so that you will not be dependent on anybody.*

13 Brothers and sisters, we do not want you to be uninformed about those who sleep in death, so that you do not grieve like the rest of mankind, who have no hope. 14 For we believe that Jesus died and rose again, and so we believe that God will bring with Jesus those who have fallen asleep in him. 15 According to the Lord's word, we tell you that we who are still alive, who are left until the coming of the Lord, will certainly not precede those who have fallen asleep. 16 For the Lord himself will come down from heaven, with a loud command, with the voice of the archangel and with the trumpet call of God, and the dead in Christ will rise first. 17 After that, we who are still alive and are left will be caught up together with them in the clouds to meet the Lord in the air. And so we will be with the Lord forever. 18 Therefore encourage one another with these words.

1. What grabbed your attention from these verses?

2. What verses or specific words do you want to understand better?

3. What words or phrases are repeated in this passage? Give verses.

4. What topics (if any) in this passage have we studied in previous lessons?

5. *Gain perspective:* From this lesson's passage (vv. 13-18), choose one verse to dwell upon all week long. Write it in the space below. Ask God to teach you through this verse.

Respond to the Lord about what you learned today.

DAY TWO STUDY

Read 1 Thessalonians 4:13-18. Ask the Lord Jesus to teach you through His Word.

Today, we will focus on what is said in verses 13-17 and try to carefully cover what it all means. Because of that, today's study will be longer than usual. Day Three Study will expand our understanding of our future life beyond death.

> **Focus on the Meaning:** The precious truth concerning the coming of Christ for His own is as certain as the central doctrine of the death and resurrection of Christ. This coming (Gr. *parousia*, lit. "appearing") of Christ is the same as His *appearing in the clouds* (Acts 1:11). It is not His Second Coming...at which time He will remain on the earth, set up His earthly kingdom, and reign for 1,000 years (Rev. 19:11-21). The differences in the descriptions of these comings present them as separate events. (*Dr. Constables Notes on 1 Thessalonians 2020 Edition,* pp. 50-51)

What does the Bible say?

6. Answer these questions based on what is written in the text.

   What did Paul not want for them (v. 13)?

   When Jesus comes, who will come with Him (v. 14)?

   From whom did Paul get this information (v. 15)?

   What is certain for those who are still alive when He comes (v. 15)?

   What recognizable events will accompany Jesus' coming (v. 16)?

   After the dead rise, what will happen (v. 17)?

   What are we to do with this information (v. 18)?

> **Scriptural Insight:** "According to the Lord's word" (v. 15) means that this information came to Paul by revelation from the Lord, not just Paul's opinion. It could have been an otherwise unrecorded saying of Christ. Or it could have come to Paul by direct revelation (cf. Acts 16:6; 18:9; 1 Cor. 2:10; 2 Cor. 12:1-4; Gal. 1:12, 16; Eph. 3:3). (*Dr. Constable's Notes on 1 Thessalonians 2020 Edition,* p. 51)

What does it mean?

The Thessalonians were apparently concerned that Christians who had died would miss the Lord's coming and gathering of believers. Paul countered this with truth for them and for us to get a glimpse of what will occur. God has chosen to give this information to us.

In verses 13-15, the Bible describes three groups of people— (1) those who have "fallen asleep," (2) those with no hope, and (3) those who are still alive when Jesus comes.

Those who have fallen asleep:

7. Jesus defined for us what "fallen asleep" means. Read John 11:11-15. When Jesus talked about Lazarus having fallen asleep, what did He mean?

8. Those who have "fallen asleep" are Christians who have died. Read 2 Corinthians 5:6-9 and Philippians 1:20-24. Summarize what you can know with confidence about what happens when a believer dies.

Focus on the Meaning: A believer falls asleep on earth and wakes up in heaven, passing from earth into the presence of the Lord. Death is like a comma between the two. We have the promise of being able to enjoy heaven and be recognizable. Based on 2 Corinthians 5:1-5, we know we will be given a heavenly body that will contain our soul until we get our new resurrected body at the time of the Rapture. One thing is for sure, we will be perfected and released from the struggle with sin through being set free from our mortal body.

9. Paul mentioned earlier in 1 Thessalonians 3:13 that Jesus would be bringing His holy ones with Him. Those are the ones who have fallen asleep in Him (v. 14), also known as the "dead in Christ" (v. 16). What will they experience?

Historical Insight: The [Romans] cremated bodies and placed the ashes in urns set in niches. These niches looked like dovecotes, so they were called *columbaria*. But the Christians used the name for the barracks of soldiers, *koimeterion*, from which we get "cemetery." Thus, at death, the believer falls asleep as at the sounding of Taps. But the angel will blow the trumpet of resurrection, just as the bugler sounds reveille. Then the dead in Christ will come out of the barracks of the dead, to be forever with their glorious Captain. (Donald Grey Barnhouse, *Romans Book VI*, p. 113)

Those who have no hope: These are the unsaved. We will cover this subject more in Lesson 9.

Those who are still alive:

10. The phrase "caught up" (v. 17, literally "snatched by force") was translated into Latin as *rapiemur* (the act of carrying off), which became *rapturo* in the medieval times. This event has been called "The Rapture" ever since. And the definition of rapture has changed to "joyful ecstasy" to match the event.

   • What will those believers who are still alive see, hear, and experience according to vv. 15-17?

   • Read Numbers 10:1-2. God commanded the silver trumpets to be used for what?

   • Read John 11:43. What do you learn from Jesus' earthly example?

   Scriptural Insight: The "loud command" was used in classical Greek for the shout with which an officer gives the order to his troops or his crew. It carries a ring of authority and a note of urgency (see John 11:43). The trumpet call was used to convene God's people to gather before Him (see Numbers 10:2). This trumpet call is not related to the seven trumpets of revelation because those are calls of judgment of God upon a Christ-rejecting world. By contrast, the trumpet call in 1 Thessalonians 4 is a call addressed to the saved, to those who have trusted in the Lord Jesus Christ. As to the angelic voice, we are not told more about this. The only archangel mentioned in Scripture is Michael (Jude 9). (Adapted from *Dr. Constable's Notes on 1 Thessalonians 2021 Edition*, pp. 53-55)

11. Read Titus 2:13. What did Paul call this event? Why was that a good choice of words?

12. From what you have learned so far, where does the believer go? See also John 14:1-3.

Scriptural Insight: All believers with their new bodies will join Jesus in the clouds and accompany Him back to heaven. Since "we will be with the Lord forever" from then on, we will go with Christ to His Father's house in heaven (John 14:2-3), return to earth with Him at His Second Coming (Revelation 19:14), participate in His earthly millennial kingdom with Him (Revelation 20:6), and finally dwell with Him in the new heavens and new earth (Revelation 21:3-4). (*Dr. Constable's Notes on 1 Thessalonians 2020 Edition*, pp. 55-56)

13. Everything that takes place with the believers at the Rapture is initiated by the Lord and done by Him. Jesus Christ acts to gather His own and transport them from earth into His presence. Going back to the concern of the Thessalonians (vv. 13-15), is it possible for any believer, including you, to miss this event we call "the Rapture?" Why or why not?

Scriptural Insight: Paul and the other early Christians believed in the imminent (about to happen) return of Christ. For them, nothing had to occur before His return. The time of the Rapture has been a matter of disagreement among conservative interpreters. What we can know for sure is that Christians are not destined to experience the outpouring of God's wrath (1:10; 5:9-10), which the Tribulation will include. There is no mention of the Tribulation in this passage, but that would be expected if it will precede the Rapture, especially since the Thessalonians were experiencing some tribulation. "Most who believe it will occur before the Tribulation base their belief on 1 Thessalonians 4:13-17 since it contains more detail about the Rapture than any other one. All conservative scholars agree that the translation of living Christians and the resurrection of dead Christians will take place at the same time. On this issue there is agreement, regardless of when the Rapture will occur in relation to the Tribulation." (*Dr. Constable's Notes on 1 Thessalonians 2021 Edition*, p. 48)

What application will you make to gain a biblical perspective?

14. As a believer, have you learned enough in this lesson to give you confidence and comfort about your death or the death of any Christian loved one? Look at the chart below to gain confidence about what happens when you die.

What doesn't happen at death	What does happen at death
• Not annihilation (Luke 16:19-31)	• Fall asleep on earth; wake up in heaven (1 Thessalonians 4:14)
• Not soul sleep (Philippians 1:23)	
• Not floating spirit (2 Cor. 5:3)	• Leave earthly tent; get heavenly dwelling fashioned for us (2 Cor. 5:1)
• Not reincarnation (Hebrews 9:27)	
• Not purgatory (Colossians 1:22)	• Be immediately at home with the lord (2 Cor. 5:8)
• Not becoming an angel (Mark 9:4)	

Think About It: How will God raise the bodies of people who were buried hundreds of years ago? What about the bodies of those Christians who were burned to death and those whose ashes were thrown to the wind, and Christians who perished at sea? ... The God who created the universe out of nothing with a word is fully able to reassemble the decayed bodies of all His saints in a moment of time (see 1 Corinthians 15:35-38). (*The Bible Knowledge Commentary New Testament,* p. 704)

15. Paul did not deny that the death of a believer brings grief to his or her loved ones. Jesus shared in his friends' grief (John 11:35). Nevertheless, Paul insisted that Christians need "not grieve" as those "who have no hope" grieve. How does knowing this glimpse into your future encourage you or give you hope in the midst of grief, suffering, or growing old?

Respond to the Lord about what you learned today.

DAY THREE STUDY

Read 1 Thessalonians 4:13-18. Ask the Lord Jesus to teach you through His Word.

What does it mean?

Today, we will expand our study of life beyond death, especially the new bodies we will receive.

16. Read Philippians 3:20-21 and 1 John 3:2-3. What will happen when Jesus appears?

Focus on the Meaning: Dead Christians will experience resurrection from the dead as their bodies are recreated by God and joined with their spirits once again. Living [Christians] will experience what Bible scholars have termed "translation," meaning "the conversion of something from one form into another." This will happen instantly as they, too, get a resurrection body but without having to experience death first. All will have immortal bodies like Christ's body. This translation of living believers is the only interpretation that fits with Jesus' statements in John 14:1-3. Then, indeed, the believers will go from earth to heaven, to the place prepared in the Father's house.

To the Greek mind, the resurrection of the body was an absurd idea. They thought that their body was evil, and only the soul was good. So death rescued the soul from the body. Their thinking was this, "Why would anyone want to have a human body again?" The Greeks thought the resurrection was foolishness. Paul continually taught that Jesus' resurrection was absolutely essential to the Christian faith (1 Corinthians 15:12-20), and it was a foretaste of what every Christian will one day experience.

17. Read Luke 24:13-45. What do you learn about Jesus' resurrection body?

18. Read 1 Corinthians 15:51-57. What do you learn about our future resurrection or translation?

19. *Deeper Discoveries (optional):* Contrast the Christian view of death and the afterlife with the views of non-Christian religions.

What the Bible teaches in 1 Thessalonians 4:13-18 and the Scriptures above are intended to encourage the readers, including you. And we are to use these same words to encourage other Christians as we are waiting for His appearing to gather us together with Him.

What application will you make to gain a biblical perspective?

20. Discuss your willingness to trust God and be content *not knowing when* Christ will appear but living as if it were today. How should you live now? Review 1 Thessalonians 3:13-4:1.

21. When you were a child, what did you imagine heaven to be like? As an adult, what do you imagine heaven to be like? Whom are you expecting/hoping to see there? Are you excited about your future? Feel free to use any creative means (poem, prose, song, drawing, craft) to describe your anticipation of this glorious event. The next page is mostly blank for this purpose. Or search online for artists' renderings of the Rapture and be inspired. ☺

Recommended: Listen to the podcast "Gain the Biblical Perspective on Death and Beyond" after doing this lesson to reinforce what you have learned. Use the listener guide on the next page.

Gain the Biblical Perspective on Death and Beyond

Trying to understand prophecy about the end times in both the Old and New Testaments is like having a bunch of puzzle pieces that look similar but without the picture on the box top to tell you how to arrange them. All we know for sure are the border pieces. We can put the 4 sides of the puzzle together. Those are events we know will definitely happen, but we don't know when or how the rest of the pieces fit inside the border.

Our lesson covered the first side: Christ appearing as Savior to gather all Christians, dead and alive, together with Him in the clouds. At the beginning of John chapter 14, Jesus declared that He was definitely, positively, you-can-count-on-it-with-certainty coming back to earth to gather all of His followers and bring them to live in heaven with Him. There's no mistake about it. If Jesus said that was going to happen, it will! After all, He promised to His followers that He would be raised from the dead after being crucified. That happened. God keeps His promises.

Through His Spirit, the Lord inspired Paul to write about this glorious event in 1 Thessalonians 4:13-17.

THE BIBLICAL PERSPECTIVE ON DEATH

- Death was not part of God's original design for us. Adam and Eve were created to live forever in a perfect environment with total freedom and everything they needed.

- God gave them only one prohibition (Genesis 2:17). Satan tempted them, they ate, and they experienced death. Immediately, they experienced spiritual death or separation from God. Their bodies began to physically die that day as well. Since then, every human is born separated from God. And physical death has been the destiny of both humans and animals.

- There was no death anywhere before Adam sinned. Death is not nature's way of ridding itself of the unfit, as evolution teaches. **Death is the penalty for sin**. It has no other reason to exist. *Romans 5:12*

- Jesus Christ paid the death penalty for sin and destroyed death's power over us. *John 1:29; 2 Timothy 1:9-10; Hebrews 2:14-15*

- Therefore, we are no longer in bondage to death. Death for the believer should hold no terror because death for us is a doorway into glory. Death is the way that we just go home.

AT DEATH, WE GO TO BE WITH THE LORD.

For simplicity's sake, we use the term "soul" to represent our personhood apart from the body (our intellect, emotions, will, and spirit).

- At death, the body decays and reunites with the earth. The soul leaves this "earthly tent" and is immediately perfected by God so that we enter heaven without any sin at all.

- The Bible teaches that the soul of a believer goes directly to the presence of the Lord. *Philippians 1:23; 2 Corinthians 5:8*

  ✓ The soul is not annihilated. That's the atheistic view.
  ✓ The soul doesn't just go to sleep and do nothing while waiting to join a future resurrected body. We will be aware of being in heaven and in God's presence.
  ✓ There is no reincarnation as the eastern religions teach.
  ✓ We don't float on clouds playing harps as the cartoons depict.
  ✓ There is no such place called purgatory where you must do penance for your sin until you are purged enough for heaven. Everything that needs to be done to get us ready for immediate entrance into heaven has been done by Jesus Christ.
  ✓ Dead Christians do not become angels in heaven.

THOSE WHO HAVE FALLEN ASLEEP IN HIM (1 THESSALONIANS 4:14)

- Those who have fallen asleep in Him are Christians who have died. Their souls are with Jesus in heaven.

- Jesus brings their souls with Him when He comes to gather His own. Every Christian who has died since Pentecost will be coming with Jesus to be reunited with a newly fashioned resurrected body.

THOSE WHO ARE STILL ALIVE AT HIS APPEARING (1 THESSALONIANS 4:17)

- The phrase "caught up" in Latin is *rapturo*. So this event has been called "the Rapture" for many years. Rapture is "the state of being transported by a lofty emotion; ecstasy." Yes, we believers will be in ecstasy to be with our Lord, to see Him with our eyes and hear His voice with our ears. We will truly be with Him. What a time of true rapture!

- We will also be instantly given new immortal bodies like Christ's resurrected body but without having to experience death first. We will join together in the clouds with those who had died and received new bodies. This may only be visible to believers—living and dead. Later, Jesus Christ will return to earth and stay on earth.

THOSE LEFT BEHIND

- Sadly, many won't experience such rapture—the ones who are left behind. But anyone who has ever heard the gospel or heard about Jesus can join the ecstasy simply by trusting in Christ now with their lives. How do we get this message out to them so they will take it seriously?

The hope of heaven transforms our perspective on death. We grieve, but we grieve not as those who have no hope, rather as those who are certain of our reunion with loved ones who have gone before, of receiving a glorious body that will never weaken or decay, of entering a wonderful new life beyond our fondest dreams, and of forever being with the Lord!

Let Jesus satisfy your heart with His perspective on life in the present and in the future. Then, live securely in Him during this time of waiting.

8: Perspective on Living in the Light

1 Thessalonians 5:1-28

DAY ONE STUDY—GET THE BIG PICTURE

Ask the Lord Jesus to teach you through His Word.

Trying to understand prophecy about the future is like having a bunch of puzzle pieces that look similar but without the picture on the box top to tell you how to arrange them. All we know for sure are the border pieces. We can put the 4 sides of the puzzle together. Those are events we know will definitely happen, but we don't know when or how the rest of the pieces fit inside the border. Paul described one such event in 1 Thessalonians chapter 4. This is Christ appearing as Savior to gather all believers, dead and alive, together with Him in the clouds. A second event is the Great Tribulation during which God's wrath against sin is directed toward earth. That is introduced to us in 1 Thessalonians chapter 5.

What does the Bible say?

Read the Bible passage below (NIV). Use your own method (colored pencils, lines, shapes) to mark 1) anything that grabs your attention, 2) words you want to understand, and 3) topics you have seen before in this letter. Draw arrows between thoughts that connect.

5 *¹ Now, brothers and sisters, about times and dates we do not need to write to you, ² for you know very well that the day of the Lord will come like a thief in the night. ³ While people are saying, "Peace and safety," destruction will come on them suddenly, as labor pains on a pregnant woman, and they will not escape.*

⁴ But you, brothers and sisters, are not in darkness so that this day should surprise you like a thief. ⁵ You are all children of the light and children of the day. We do not belong to the night or to the darkness. ⁶ So then, let us not be like others, who are asleep, but let us be awake and sober. ⁷ For those who sleep, sleep at night, and those who get drunk, get drunk at night. ⁸ But since we belong to the day, let us be sober, putting on faith and love as a breastplate, and the hope of salvation as a helmet. ⁹ For God did not appoint us to suffer wrath but to receive salvation through our Lord Jesus Christ. ¹⁰ He died for us so that, whether we are awake or asleep, we may live together with him. ¹¹ Therefore encourage one another and build each other up, just as in fact you are doing.

¹² Now we ask you, brothers and sisters, to acknowledge those who work hard among you, who care for you in the Lord and who admonish you. ¹³ Hold them in the highest regard in love because of their work. Live in peace with each other. ¹⁴ And we urge you, brothers and sisters, warn those who are idle and disruptive, encourage the disheartened, help the weak, be patient with everyone. ¹⁵ Make sure that nobody pays back wrong for wrong, but always strive to do what is good for each other and for everyone else.

¹⁶ Rejoice always, ¹⁷ pray continually, ¹⁸ give thanks in all circumstances; for this is God's will for you in Christ Jesus. ¹⁹ Do not quench the Spirit. ²⁰ Do not treat prophecies with contempt ²¹ but test them all; hold on to what is good, ²² reject every kind of evil.

²³ May God himself, the God of peace, sanctify you through and through. May your whole spirit, soul and body be kept blameless at the coming of our Lord Jesus Christ. ²⁴ The one who calls you is faithful, and he will do it. ²⁵ Brothers and sisters, pray for us. ²⁶ Greet all God's people with a holy kiss. ²⁷ I charge you before the Lord to have this letter read to all the brothers and sisters. ²⁸ The grace of our Lord Jesus Christ be with you.

1. What grabbed your attention from these verses?

2. What verses or specific words do you want to understand better?

3. What words or phrases are repeated in this passage? Give verses.

4. What topics (if any) in this passage have we studied in previous lessons?

5. *Gain perspective:* From this lesson's passage (5:1-28), choose one verse to dwell upon all week long. Write it in the space below. Ask God to teach you through this verse.

Respond to the Lord about what you learned today.

DAY TWO STUDY

Read 1 Thessalonians 5:1-28. Ask the Lord Jesus to teach you through His Word.

> **Scriptural Insight:** "The day of the Lord" refers to a future time in which God will be more directly and dramatically involved in world affairs than He has been since the earthly ministry of the Lord Jesus Christ. That day begins immediately after the Rapture of the church, includes the Lord's judgment against sin (Revelation 6-18), and ends with the conclusion of the Millennial Kingdom (Revelation 20). In the New Testament, the phrase "the last days" for Christians refers to that time period between Christ's ascension and His appearing to gather His own (at the Rapture). (*The Bible Knowledge Commentary New Testament*, p. 705)

What does it mean?

We will cover vv. 1-3 in the next two lessons. Today, we will focus on vv. 4-11.

This is a section about identity—to whom/what you belong and give allegiance. Paul used a lot of imagery contrasts (night/day, sleep/awake) to help us understand what it means to live according to your identity in this time until Jesus comes for us.

> **Focus on the Meaning:** "Darkness" was a common negative figure in antiquity. In the Old and New Testaments, it describes those who are ignorant of or opposed to the Lord (Ps. 82:5; Prov. 4:19; Rom. 13:12). It also describes life apart from God (John 3:19; 8:12). (*Dr. Constable's Notes on 1 Thessalonians 2020 Edition*, p. 69)

6. Unbelievers live in the kingdom of darkness (John 1:5), and "the god of this age has blinded the minds of unbelievers, so that they cannot see the light of the gospel that displays the glory of Christ, who is the image of God" (2 Corinthians 4:4). According to the following verses, what has God done for believers to rescue us from that condition?

    • 2 Corinthians 4:6—

    • Colossians 1:13—

7. Because of this rescue...

    • What is now our identity (1 Thessalonians 5:5)?

    • As children of the light/day, what state of mind should we maintain regarding daily life (v. 6) See also Mark 13:32-37.

8. The word Paul used that is translated "awake" (v. 6) means to be alert, not insensible. His word translated "sober" means to be calm and collected in spirit, to not be drunk.

   - With those definitions in mind, what would it look like in a believer's life to be "awake and sober?" See also Ephesians 5:8-11.

   - What would the opposite look like (v. 7)?

   Focus on the Meaning: The Lord Jesus does not come to the church like a thief in the night. The church is looking for and waiting for the Lord to come. ... However, the Lord Jesus does come like a thief to the world after the church has been raptured. (*Dr. Constable's Notes on 1 Thessalonians 2020 Edition*, p. 65)

9. While being awake and sober, what else are we to do (v. 8) and how would that help us live through times of suffering like the Thessalonians were experiencing?

   Scriptural Insight: Paul didn't invent the armor analogy. God did. See Isaiah 59:15-17. When the Lord saw the need, He acted. Notice the armor He put on to meet the challenge. Paul built on God's example and applied it to Christians putting on God's armor, first here in 1 Thessalonians then more expanded in Ephesians 6:10-17. It is all still God's armor we are wearing. He gives it to us to wear.

10. In verses 9-10, what comfort did Paul give to the Thessalonian believers in the anticipation of the coming "day of the Lord?"

There are two aspects of God's wrath in the New Testament: (1) His anger against sin (Romans 1:18) and (2) the judgment of God on the unbelieving world during the Tribulation. Jesus' sacrifice on the cross appeased God's anger against sin for anyone who trusts in Christ. Therefore, every Christian is already saved from God's general wrath against sin. All Christians are also promised in 1 Thessalonians 5:9 and 1:10 that we will be delivered from the wrath to come. Both of these verses are strong evidence that believers will be raptured before the Great Tribulation described in Revelation 6-19.

Scriptural Insight: That's how God worked in His other times of judgment. In Genesis chapter 7, God told Noah and his family when to get in the Ark for their safety. After they were safely out of the way, He brought the judgment of the Flood. In Genesis chapter 19, God sent angels to rescue Lot and his family out of Sodom. As soon as they were safely out of the way, He brought the judgment of fire. Jesus confirmed that pattern in Luke 17:26-30 and said that God's plan for us is the same.

11. Why would knowing the truths about the appearing of the Lord for His own be reason to "encourage one another and build each other up" (v. 11)?

Focus on the Meaning: Paul's words in 1 Thessalonians 5:10 could refer to those believers who are alive or dead as well as those who are watchful or not watchful (spiritually lazy) Regardless, it is clear that Jesus will snatch away all Christians at the Rapture. He initiates and carries it out. Not one believer will be forgotten and left behind. This certainly feeds our hope!

What application will you make to gain a biblical perspective?

12. Were you raised with the misconception that you couldn't be holy enough to escape God's wrath? What have you learned that convinces you what you were taught is not true?

13. Christians often fill their time with church activities and surround themselves with church friends. Over time, this may develop a critical "stay away from me" attitude towards the unbelievers around us. But we all know those who do not believe in Christ, maybe in your own family, workplace, and neighborhood.

   • Why should you have compassion on those who have not experienced God's grace?

   • Consider just one non-Christian woman in your life right now. Ask Jesus to give you His love and compassion for her and to help you understand what she is feeling and needing from Him. How can you make the most of your connection to build a relationship with her so that you can show Jesus' love and compassion to her?

Respond to the Lord about what you learned today.

DAY THREE STUDY

Read 1 Thessalonians 5:1-28. Ask the Lord Jesus to teach you through His Word.

What does it mean?

Today, we will focus on vv. 12-28.

In vv. 12-15, we see application of v. 11 in community with other believers. Believers live in a unique relationship with one another. We have a common destiny and a mutual responsibility to each other. But these behaviors also shine light into darkness for unbelievers who are watching us.

14. Paul first addressed our responsibility to our spiritual leaders.

   • How should you treat your spiritual leaders (vv. 12-13)? See also 1 Timothy 5:17-19.

   • How would these actions encourage believers and shine light for unbelievers?

   Scriptural Insight: Clearly there were teachers in the Thessalonian church, even though it was a new church. We may assume, therefore, that the apostles had appointed leaders in this church before they departed from Thessalonica, as they had done in the churches of Galatia (cf. Acts 14:23). These leaders were probably Jews who had a solid background in the Hebrew Bible and had come to faith in Christ. (*Dr. Constable's Notes on 1 Thessalonians 2020 Edition*, p. 73)

15. ***Deeper Discoveries (optional):*** Research other verses that describe the work of our spiritual shepherds and what our response should be to them. Start with Acts 20:28-32.

Paul then addressed our responsibility to other members of the Body of Christ.

16. Looking at v. 14. "Idle and disruptive" translates a Greek word meaning unruly, undisciplined. We will cover this again in Lesson 11.

   • What are the instructions to believers? See also 1 Thessalonians 4:11-12.

   • How would these actions encourage believers and shine light for unbelievers?

17. Looking at v. 15:

- What are the instructions to believers?

- How would these actions encourage believers and shine light for unbelievers?

In vv. 16-22, we see more application of v. 5 (being children of the light) but this time from a personal spiritual life perspective. The commands in vv. 16-18 transcend all cultures at all times! These are all God's will for you in Christ Jesus (v. 18). As you consider each one, look throughout 1 Thessalonians for Paul's examples.

18. Rejoice always (v. 16). Note: this is one of ~70 New Testament commands to "Rejoice!"

- In whom or what should you rejoice? See also Philippians 4:4 and 1 Thessalonians 1:6.

- In what practical ways can you add rejoicing to your life?

19. Pray continually (v. 17). The imagery described by the Greek adverb translated "continually" is that of a lingering cough. It's not constant but frequent. See how often Paul interjects prayer throughout his letter. In what practical ways can you do this?

Dependent Living: If we live in this way, conscious continually of our dependence on God, conscious of His presence with us always, conscious of His will to bless, then our general spirit of prayerfulness will in the most natural way overflow into uttered prayer. It is instructive to read again and again in Paul's letters the many prayers that he interjects. Prayer was as natural to Paul as breathing. At any time, he was likely to break off his argument or to sum it up by some prayer of greater or less length. In the same way, our lives can be lived in such an attitude of dependence on God that we will easily and naturally move into the words of prayer on all sorts of occasions, great and small, grave and [happy]. Prayer is to be constant. (*Dr. Constable's Notes on 1 Thessalonians 2020 Edition*, p. 76)

20. Give thanks in all circumstances (v. 18), not necessarily "for" all circumstances. In what practical ways can you do this?

21. Do not quench the Spirit (v. 19). One of the biblical symbols for the Holy Spirit is "fire." No believer can fully extinguish the Holy Spirit's fire inside you. But the word "quench" can also mean to stifle or suppress the fire's influence. What would it look like to quench (stifle or suppress) the work of the Spirit in your life? See also 1 Thessalonians 3:3,5 and 4:4-6, 8.

Dependent Living: Believers can hinder the work of the Holy Spirit in their lives by living as self-reliant, independent-of-God creatures. Although we can resist His work, that doesn't stop His work to conform us to the image of Christ (Romans 8:29; 2 Corinthians 3:18). Because that is His goal, He may bring things into our lives that force us to depend on God more than on ourselves (2 Corinthians 1:9). As Paul wrote in Philippians 1:6, what God started in us, He will complete. We can cooperate with the Spirit by yielding to His work and letting Him transform us (Romans 12:1-2).

22. Looking at vv. 20-22, Paul referred to prophecies.

Focus on the Meaning: The New Testament gift of prophecy was the ability to receive and communicate direct revelations from God before the New Testament was completed. The testing of what was revealed through speaking or writing resulted in our New Testament canon. Those writings have been authenticated, along with the entire Old Testament, to be God's prophetic teaching to all of us. All of it is good. A modern application of this "testing" can be directed toward any current teaching claiming to be divinely inspired and declaring the purposes of God.

- Regarding that which has already passed the test to be considered God's Word, how are we to respond? See John 8:31-32; 1 Thessalonians 2:12; 4:8; and 2 Timothy 3:16-17.

- Regarding modern teaching that claims to be truth from God, what are we to do with it? How would you do that?

23. Read vv. 23-24 again. To sanctify means to set apart from anything evil, to make holy as God is holy and separate from evil. See also 1 Thessalonians 3:13.

- What will the God of peace do for all of us?

- How does this truth encourage you and feed your hope?

24. ***Deeper Discoveries (optional):*** Compare how Paul ended this letter with how he ended other letters to churches. Read these verses, which are listed in chronological order. Galatians 6:18; 1 Thessalonians 5:25-28; 2 Thessalonians 3:16-18; 1 Corinthians 16:19-24; 2 Corinthians 13:12-14; Ephesians 6:23-24; Philippians 4:21-23; and Colossians 4:16-18. What similarities do you notice? What helped people to know these were genuinely from Paul?

What application will you make to gain a biblical perspective?

25. Review how we are to live as children of the light (vv. 6, 8, 11, 13-22). If you have those verses firmly entrenched in your life, what impact would that make on …

- Your personal spiritual life?

- Your life in the community of Christ (especially your local church)?

- Persecution you may face?

- Drawing nonbelievers to Christ who are in your sphere of influence?

Pray 1 Thessalonians 5:23 for yourself and others.

Recommended: Listen to the podcast "Gain the Biblical Perspective on Shining God's Light" after doing this lesson to reinforce what you have learned. Use the listener guide on the next page.

Gain the Biblical Perspective on Shining God's Light

THE DAY OF THE LORD

- The day of the Lord" refers to a future time in which God will be more directly and dramatically involved in world affairs than He has been since the earthly ministry of the Lord Jesus Christ. That day begins after the Rapture of the church, includes the Lord's judgment against sin in what is called the Great Tribulation (Revelation chapters 6-18), Christ's Second Coming in blazing fire (Revelation chapter 19), and ends with the conclusion of the "Millennial Kingdom" and final judgments of those who reject Christ (Revelation chapter 20).

- Concerning the Great Tribulation, we won't be on earth at that time. We are promised salvation and rescue from God's wrath in 1 Thessalonians 1:10 and 5:9. And that's how God worked in His other times of judgment. *Genesis 7; Genesis 19; Luke 17:26-30*

- If we won't be here to witness it, and we have no actual control over what will happen, then why did the Lord give us so much detail about that time? All Scripture is useful for teaching and rebuking (2 Timothy 3:16-17). All the verses describing what will happen during the Great Tribulation are a warning to those who reject the Gospel message now. Another purpose is to teach Christians how to live now in order to draw unbelievers to Jesus so they will believe and be saved. The purpose is not so we will spend our lives trying to figure out how all the puzzle pieces fit together. Only God knows that picture.

- Until He appears, we are supposed to be waiting for Him, ready for His appearing. *1 Thessalonians 5:4-6*

  God doesn't work on our timetable. He has a plan that He will execute perfectly and for the highest, greatest good of all, and for His ultimate glory. (Chuck Swindoll)

- We all have good intentions to share our faith with others if they ask us. God's love should compel us to share the gospel truth. If we are God's messengers, we need to be living as someone who shines light to those in darkness.

LIVING AS SOMEONE WHO SHINES LIGHT IN THE DARKNESS

You are all children of the light and children of the day. We do not belong to the night or to the darkness. So then, let us not be like others, who are asleep, but let us be awake and sober. (1 Thessalonians 5:5-6)

- Believers in Jesus Christ are children of the light. You are no longer in the kingdom of darkness. You are in the kingdom of light. It's a new identity. Live as children of the light.

- Your faith and love for God is a breastplate protecting your heart from corrupting influences. Your hope in your salvation and belief in Christ's promise to come for you is like a helmet protecting your mind from doubt and despair. Those flow from your identity as children of the light.

- Your identity as children of the light is visible to others. Most of the rest of chapter 5 describes all the ways you can live your life as children of the light. And each one of these provides light to watching unbelievers.

  - ✓ Encourage and build each other up (v. 11)
  - ✓ Esteem and love your spiritual leaders (vv. 12-13)
  - ✓ Live in peace with each other (v. 13)
  - ✓ Warn those who are idle and disruptive (v. 14)
  - ✓ Encourage those who are disheartened (v. 14)
  - ✓ Help the weak (v. 14)
  - ✓ Be patient with everyone (v. 14)
  - ✓ Don't pay back wrong for wrong (v. 15)
  - ✓ Strive to do what is good for each other and for everyone else (v. 15)
  - ✓ Rejoice always (v. 16)
  - ✓ Pray continually (v. 17)
  - ✓ Give thanks in all circumstances (v. 18)
  - ✓ Don't quench the Spirit (v. 19)
  - ✓ Test all teachings to hold onto what is good and reject what is evil (vv. 20-22)

- All of these are God's will for your life. But the best news is that He doesn't expect you to do this on your own. God Himself will sanctify you. *1 Thessalonians 5:23-24*

- The word *sanctify* means to be set apart from sin and to God. By faith in Jesus Christ, God declares us holy in His sight. We are clothed with Christ (Galatians 3:27).

- You are also being made holy in your thoughts, words, and actions by the work of the Holy Spirit. This is ongoing from the moment of salvation until the Lord comes or you die, when your "being made holy" is complete.

- It is Christ at work in you through His Spirit that enables you to do anything good in His name—whether for yourself or for anyone else. We are to live dependently on Him to do this. *Colossians 1:29; Philippians 1:6*

- You can always pray to the Lord like this: "Lord Jesus, I can't do this on my own. I trust you to do this in me and through me." Then, watch what He does!

The New Testament teaches that Jesus' return for us could be at any time. Yes, it has been just shy of 2000 years of waiting. But if we lived as though we believed that to be true, and asked Jesus to give us His heart's compassion for the unbelievers around us, how would that affect our lives today? Would we be more interested in shining the light rather than just contentedly dancing in the light with our friends?

Let Jesus satisfy your heart with His perspective on life in the present and in the future. Then, live securely in Him during this time of waiting.

9: Perspective on God's Justice

2 Thessalonians 1:1-12

Historical Insight: A few months after the Thessalonians received Paul's first letter, someone reported news of the church back to Paul. The good news was that most of the Thessalonians were growing in their faith and love for each other in spite of persecution. But there still seemed to be confusion about "the day of the Lord." Also, the expectation of the Lord's imminent return had caused some to quit their jobs and just "wait." Being confused as well as idle is never a good combination for people, even Christians. So Paul wrote the letter called 2 Thessalonians within 6-12 months of the first one. Chronologically, it is Paul's third letter in our New Testament, assuming Galatians was his first.

DAY ONE STUDY—GET THE BIG PICTURE

Trying to understand prophecy about the future is like having a bunch of puzzle pieces that look similar but without the picture on the box top to tell you how to arrange them. All we know for sure are the border pieces. We can put the 4 sides of the puzzle together. Those are events we know will definitely happen, but we don't know when or how the rest of the pieces fit inside the border. We have looked at two events in our study so far. Another event is introduced to us in 2 Thessalonians chapter 1. It is Christ coming in judgment on unbelievers and setting up His kingdom on earth.

Ask the Lord Jesus to teach you through His Word.

What does the Bible say?

Let's start digging into this wonderful letter from God to us. Read the Bible passage below (NIV) including verses from the last lesson. Use your own method (colored pencils, lines, shapes) to mark 1) anything that grabs your attention, 2) words you want to understand, and 3) topics you have seen before in this letter. Draw arrows between thoughts that connect.

5 *23 May God himself, the God of peace, sanctify you through and through. May your whole spirit, soul and body be kept blameless at the coming of our Lord Jesus Christ. 24 The one who calls you is faithful, and he will do it. 25 Brothers and sisters, pray for us. 26 Greet all God's people with a holy kiss. 27 I charge you before the Lord to have this letter read to all the brothers and sisters. 28 The grace of our Lord Jesus Christ be with you.*

1 *Paul, Silas and Timothy,*

To the church of the Thessalonians in God our Father and the Lord Jesus Christ:

2 Grace and peace to you from God the Father and the Lord Jesus Christ.

3 We ought always to thank God for you, brothers and sisters, and rightly so, because your faith is growing more and more, and the love all of you have for one another is increasing. 4 Therefore, among God's churches we boast about your perseverance and faith in all the persecutions and trials you are enduring.

5 All this is evidence that God's judgment is right, and as a result you will be counted worthy of the kingdom of God, for which you are suffering. 6 God is just: He will pay back trouble to those who trouble you 7 and give relief to you who are troubled, and to us as well. This will happen when the Lord Jesus is revealed from heaven in blazing fire with his powerful angels. 8 He will punish those *who do not know God and do not obey the gospel of our Lord Jesus. ⁹ They will be punished with everlasting destruction and shut out from the presence of the Lord and from the glory of his might ¹⁰ on the day he comes to be glorified in his holy people and to be marveled at among all those who have believed. This includes you, because you believed our testimony to you.*

¹¹ With this in mind, we constantly pray for you, that our God may make you worthy of his calling, and that by his power he may bring to fruition your every desire for goodness and your every deed prompted by faith. ¹² We pray this so that the name of our Lord Jesus may be glorified in you, and you in him, according to the grace of our God and the Lord Jesus Christ.

1. What grabbed your attention from these verses?

2. What verses or specific words do you want to understand better?

3. What words or phrases are repeated in this passage? Give verses.

4. What topics (if any) in this passage have we studied in previous lessons?

5. **Gain perspective:** From this lesson's passage (1:1-12), choose one verse to dwell upon all week long. Write it in the space below. Ask God to teach you through this verse.

Respond to the Lord about what you learned today.

DAY TWO STUDY

Read 2 Thessalonians 1:1-12. Ask the Lord Jesus to teach you through His Word.

Today, we will focus on vv. 5-10. This section deals with God's judgment and justice.

What does it mean?

> **Focus on the Meaning:** God is just. To be just means that you are always doing what is morally right and fair. Our God always acts with justice. It is the natural expression of His holiness. Remember we said that God's holiness always sets Him apart from anything that is sinful or evil. The Bible says that God hates sin and has declared that sin is wrong and must be punished by death. Jesus paid the penalty for sin that God's justice demands. The word translated "judgment" in v. 5 means "separating out." God separates the saved from the ones who reject Him.

6. In 2 Thessalonians 1:5, Paul declared that God's judgment is right. The Thessalonians would be counted worthy of God's kingdom. Read Romans 3:21-26. On what basis does God declare anyone worthy of His kingdom?

> **Think About It:** God called us and counted us worthy in Christ before the process of making us worthy in Christ is completed.

7. In v. 6 (and 1 Thessalonians 4:6), Paul described our just God acting in the role of an Avenger.

   • What does an avenger do?

   • How will our just God act as an avenger (vv. 6-7, first part)?

   • When will this happen for sure (v. 7)?

> **Scriptural Insight:** Powerful angels and blazing fire represent judgment. This return of Christ is not the Rapture as described in 1 Thessalonians 4:14-17, which is for Christians and completes their salvation from all of God's wrath (1 Thessalonians 5:9). This is the Second Coming of Jesus Christ at the end of the Great Tribulation (Revelation 19). This is not a reference to the Rapture.

8. Why should knowing that God will avenge wrongs done to believers give relief to the Thessalonians (and to us).

Focus on the Meaning: Although God will act as avenger during His judgment on unbelievers in the future, He could and does act as avenger for us in our lifetimes.

In Lesson 8, we learned that "the day of the Lord" refers to a future time in which God will be more directly and dramatically involved in world affairs than He has been since the earthly ministry of the Lord Jesus Christ. That day begins immediately after the Rapture of the church, includes the Lord's wrath against sin (Revelation 6-18), Christ's Second Coming in blazing fire (Revelation 19), and ends with the conclusion of His Millennial Kingdom (Revelation 20).

9. Read 1 Thessalonians 5:2-3 and Matthew 24:36-39.

   * What is the warning?

   * Has God been faithful to warn mankind about impending judgment in the past?

   * Is there any real reason not to heed His warning of coming judgment on the unbelieving world?

10. According to 2 Thessalonians 1:8, God's judgment falls on whom? See also Acts 17:30-31 and Romans 1:18-20.

Think About It: The Rapture removes God's representatives from earth at once. The unbelievers left behind will for a short time experience what they want—being away from the knowledge and presence of God. Yet, God will use the time of judgment to draw more people to Him in faith by sending witnesses (Revelation 11). Even in judgment, He is good.

God makes His offer of amnesty to all humans so easy. God has done everything possible to communicate to every human that He exists and loves them. The Gospel is the Lord's message of hope and salvation. The only stipulation is that you must personally accept the message through faith in Jesus Christ. Just believe in His Son Jesus Christ. Yet, human arrogance and independence prefers to turn away from the enormous treasure they would have in Jesus Christ. Sadly, many refuse God's gracious offer. Those who reject Christ will, in turn, experience God's rejection and the loss of everything worthwhile in life. It is their choice of destiny. Every human is an immortal being. You are a soul. You have a body. Once your body dies, your soul continues. It is not annihilated at death as the atheists teach.

11. How did Paul describe eternal hell in verse 9?

> **Focus on the Meaning:** [All] non-Christians will suffer, literally "pay a penalty," of "eternal destruction." Their fate is eternal separation from the person of Christ ("presence of the Lord") and from the manifestation of His "glory." It is not reincarnation. This is Paul's most explicit reference to the eternal duration of unbelievers' judgment in all his writings. Those who reject Christ will, in turn, experience God's rejection ... separation from God and loss of everything worthwhile in life. (*Dr. Constable's Notes on 2 Thessalonians 2020 Edition*, p. 11)

Do you have a problem accepting the reality of hell? The Bible consistently teaches this to be the destiny for the unbeliever—for everyone who rejects God's goodness and His grace given to anyone who puts their faith in Jesus Christ (v. 8). God sends no one to hell. Every individual who rejects God is making that choice for themselves.

12. ***Deeper Discoveries (optional):*** Jesus talked about hell and judgment more than anyone else in the Bible. It was the penalty for sin (Romans 6:23). He came to pay that penalty for sin. Use a concordance to find references in the gospels to hell, or go to gotquestions.org and type in the question "Does hell exist?"

13. Considering all Christians at His Second Coming (those already raptured and returning with Him or those alive on earth when He comes down), what will be our response to Jesus being our avenger (v. 10)?

> **Think About It:** The idea is that the glory of that day [Jesus' Second Coming] will far surpass anything of which we can have any idea before we behold it, and when we do behold it, we shall be lost in amazement. (*Dr. Constable's Notes on 2 Thessalonians 2020 Edition*, p. 12)

What application will you make to gain perspective?

14. How should this information impact your concern for the unbeliever? Does it?

> **Think About It:** Every wicked person can become a saved person through faith in Jesus Christ. The opportunity is available to them until their dying breath.

15. Though we can sure that God will at a future time avenge wrongs done to us, that doesn't preclude Him acting as an avenger for us today. Have you recognized a time when God acted as your avenger? Describe what happened and how you felt.

Respond to the Lord about what you learned today.

DAY THREE STUDY

Read 2 Thessalonians 1:1-12. Ask the Lord Jesus to teach you through His Word.

What does it mean?

Today, we will focus on vv. 1-4, 11-12. This is addressed to believers alive while waiting for Christ.

16. Read 1 Thessalonians 3:12-13 then read 2 Thessalonians 1:3. How had God answered Paul's prayers for the Thessalonian Christians?

> **Think About It:** The phrase concerning their faith "growing more and more" in the Greek means to grow exceedingly large and tall like trees by a wilderness stream. The word for their love "increasing" means to spread out like a flood. Aren't those beautiful work pictures? God will always answer those prayers. Asking for your faith and love to grow is in His will. Asking for perseverance during trials is also in His will. He will say, "Yes!"

17. Paul boasted about their perseverance (v. 4).

> **Focus on the Meaning:** The Greek word translated "perseverance" (v. 4) is a strong word that means "bearing under." It's holding up a load with staying power and stick-to-it-iveness. Our English word *perseverance* means "holding to a course of action, a belief, or a purpose without giving way." It is the quality that enables a person to stand on her feet when facing a storm head on. It carries the idea of whole life experience, not just getting stuck in traffic. It means staying faithful no matter what.

- Considering the Thessalonians, what were they experiencing?

- What had they not done? See 1 Thessalonians 3:3-5.

- Why would their staying faithful to Christ through suffering have encouraged Paul? See also 1 Thessalonians 3:7.

18. Read 2 Thessalonians 1:11-12. Keeping in mind what will take place in our future, we can pray for each other concerning how to live now in the waiting. For what did Paul pray (v. 11)?

What application will you make to gain perspective?

19. God's will for us is to be like Christ—to be perfect as He is perfect. That involves His part of transforming us and our part of response. According to v. 11, God's power can bring to fruition what we desire to have and do for Him as we are becoming more like Christ. Our part is having the desires for goodness and wanting to do the deeds prompted by faith that make us more like Christ. Then, asking the Lord to make those happen in our lives. This is also His will. He will say "yes" to this prayer.

His part:

- Read Romans 8:29; 2 Corinthians 3:18; and Philippians 1:6. This is God's part. What will He do?

Your part:

- What are your "desires for goodness?"

- What "deeds prompted by faith" would you like to do?

- Ask the Lord Jesus to use His power to bring to fruition those desires for goodness and deeds prompted by your faith in Him.

Scriptural Insight: Paul consistently made what God has done for believers the basis of his appeals for them to lead lives in keeping with their destiny. Christians do not live worthily in order to obtain salvation but because they have been granted salvation. (*The Bible Knowledge Commentary New Testament,* p. 716)

20. As you respond to God's work in your life, what will be the result (v. 12)?

Pray 2 Thessalonians 1:11-12 for yourself and others.

> *Recommended: Listen to the podcast "Gain the Biblical Perspective on God's Justice and Mercy" after doing this lesson to reinforce what you have learned. Use the listener guide on the next page.*

Gain the Biblical Perspective on God's Justice and Mercy

From our study of 1 and 2 Thessalonians, it is easy to become frightened by the descriptions of blazing fire, the day of the Lord, everlasting destruction, and the man of lawlessness. But God's promises of security and protection and comfort to us as believers in His Son are like a child's blanket wrapped around us. We can feel safe and snug in Him.

God offers that same blanket of protection to every human on the face of this planet. But a time comes when those who refuse His protection will get to live out the choice they have made. That is so evidently clear in 2 Thessalonians chapter 1.

WARNINGS TO THOSE WHO REFUSE GOD'S GRACE

- Our God is just. To be just means that you are always doing what is morally right and fair. Our God always acts with justice. It is the natural expression of His holiness. Remember we said that God's holiness always sets Him apart from anything that is sinful or evil. The Bible says that God hates sin and has declared that sin is wrong and must be punished by death. Jesus paid the penalty for sin that God's justice demands. The gospel offers salvation from this penalty to everyone who trusts in Him for their salvation.

- Sadly, many refuse God's gracious offer. Those who reject Christ will, in turn, experience God's rejection and the loss of everything worthwhile in life.

   They perish because they refused to love the truth and so be saved. (2 Thessalonians 2:10)

- God makes His offer of amnesty to all humans so easy. Just believe in His Son Jesus Christ. Yet, human arrogance and independence prefers to turn away from the enormous treasure they would have in Jesus Christ. It is their choice. *Romans 1:18-23*

- God has done everything possible to communicate to every human that He exists and loves them. The Gospel is the Lord's message of hope and salvation. The only stipulation is that you must personally accept the message through faith in Jesus Christ.

SECURITY FOR THOSE WHO ACCEPT GOD'S GRACE

- The good news for all believers is that we are saved from God's wrath by our faith in Jesus Christ. *Ephesians 2:8-9; 1 Thessalonians 5:9*

- That's God's mercy. Mercy is not getting what you deserve. Our sin was awful. We deserved death. But God's mercy was greater. We receive a complete pardon and life by faith in Jesus Christ. We have nothing to fear in our future. When the terrible day of the Lord begins, we who know the Lord now will not experience it. We will have been rescued ahead of time. Jesus made that promise to us. Wrap yourself up in that blanket. Stop fretting over the end times.

- But we will get to see that day when Jesus Christ returns to earth with His powerful angels to enact justice on an unbelieving rebellious world. We'll be with Him at that time. It will be glorious. Absolutely glorious. *2 Thessalonians 1:10*

- Everything you have imagined about Jesus the King coming to defeat all His enemies and truly reign over planet Earth will come to pass. You and I will see it. We are the holy people who will be with Him, marveling at King Jesus in His glory and might. Revelation 19:11-21 describe this event. We are part of His army of heaven (v. 14) as He returns, wearing the armor of God, and we will be part of His reign over planet Earth.

- In light of this glorious future, knowing that so many are still unsaved, we need to be light-bearers to those around us who don't know Him.

With this in mind, we constantly pray for you, that our God may make you worthy of his calling, and that by his power he may bring to fruition your every desire for goodness and your every deed prompted by faith. We pray this so that the name of our Lord Jesus may be glorified in you, and you in him, according to the grace of our God and the Lord Jesus Christ. (2 Thessalonians 1:11-12)

- Pray this for yourself.
  - ✓ "With this in mind"—Consider the terrible destiny for those who do not know God and refuse to accept the Gospel message. Be an intentional light-bearer to them. It's not a time for idleness, just waiting for Jesus to come. It's a time for deliberate action prompted by love.
  - ✓ "With this in mind"—Consider the glorious destiny for those who know God and have accepted His Gospel message. Desire goodness and deeds prompted by faith so that your life pleases God. Why not? You have nothing to lose and everything to gain.

Let Jesus satisfy your heart with His perspective on life in the present and in the future. Then, live securely in Him during this time of waiting.

10: Perspective on the Great Tribulation

2 Thessalonians 2:1-17

DAY ONE STUDY—GET THE BIG PICTURE

Trying to understand prophecy about the future is like having a bunch of puzzle pieces that look similar but without the picture on the box top to tell you how to arrange them. All we know for sure are the border pieces. We can put the 4 sides of the puzzle together. Those are events we know will definitely happen, but we don't know when or how the rest of the pieces fit inside the border.

We have been introduced to three events in our study so far—the Rapture, the wrath of God in the Tribulation, and Christ's second coming to judge unbelievers and set up His kingdom on earth. We will see a fourth event in this lesson—the revealing of the "man of lawlessness" (Antichrist).

Ask the Lord Jesus to teach you through His Word.

What does the Bible say?

Read the Bible passage below (NIV). Use your own method (colored pencils, lines, shapes) to mark 1) anything that grabs your attention, 2) words you want to understand, and 3) topics you have seen before in this letter. Draw arrows between thoughts that connect.

2 *¹ Concerning the coming of our Lord Jesus Christ and our being gathered to him, we ask you, brothers and sisters, ² not to become easily unsettled or alarmed by the teaching allegedly from us—whether by a prophecy or by word of mouth or by letter—asserting that the day of the Lord has already come. ³ Don't let anyone deceive you in any way, for that day will not come until the rebellion occurs and the man of lawlessness is revealed, the man doomed to destruction. ⁴ He will oppose and will exalt himself over everything that is called God or is worshiped, so that he sets himself up in God's temple, proclaiming himself to be God.*

⁵ Don't you remember that when I was with you I used to tell you these things? ⁶ And now you know what is holding him back, so that he may be revealed at the proper time. ⁷ For the secret power of lawlessness is already at work; but the one who now holds it back will continue to do so till he is taken out of the way. ⁸ And then the lawless one will be revealed, whom the Lord Jesus will overthrow with the breath of his mouth and destroy by the splendor of his coming. ⁹ The coming of the lawless one will be in accordance with how Satan works. He will use all sorts of displays of power through signs and wonders that serve the lie, ¹⁰ and all the ways that wickedness deceives those who are perishing. They perish because they refused to love the truth and so be saved. ¹¹ For this reason God sends them a powerful delusion so that they will believe the lie ¹² and so that all will be condemned who have not believed the truth but have delighted in wickedness.

¹³ But we ought always to thank God for you, brothers and sisters loved by the Lord, because God chose you as firstfruits to be saved through the sanctifying work of the Spirit and through belief in the truth. ¹⁴ He called you to this through our gospel, that you might share in the glory of our Lord Jesus Christ.

¹⁵ So then, brothers and sisters, stand firm and hold fast to the teachings we passed on to you, whether by word of mouth or by letter.

¹⁶ May our Lord Jesus Christ himself and God our Father, who loved us and by his grace gave us eternal encouragement and good hope, ¹⁷ encourage your hearts and strengthen you in every good deed and word.

1. What grabbed your attention from these verses?

2. What verses or specific words do you want to understand better?

3. What words or phrases are repeated in this passage? Give verses.

4. What topics (if any) in this passage have we previously studied in 1 or 2 Thessalonians?

5. ***Gain perspective:*** From this lesson's passage (2:1-17), choose one verse to dwell upon all week long. Write it in the space below. Ask God to teach you through this verse.

Respond to the Lord about what you learned today.

DAY TWO STUDY

Read 2 Thessalonians 2:1-17. Ask the Lord Jesus to teach you through His Word.

What does it mean?

Today, we are going to focus on vv. 1-12. Remember that these letters were written 40 years before the book of Revelation and 20 years before the destruction of the temple in Jerusalem.

> **Scriptural Insight:** "The coming of our Lord Jesus Christ" and "our gathering together to Him" both refer to the Rapture of the church. Paul had used the term "the coming" (*parousia*) of the Lord four times in 1 Thessalonians (2:19; 3:13; 4:15; 5:23), and in every case, it refers to the Rapture. "Our gathering together to Him" also refers to ... the Rapture. ... The "day of the Lord" is a time of God's judgment and wrath against evil. It includes the Tribulation, the Millennium, and the Great White Throne. (*Dr. Constable's Notes on 2 Thessalonians 2020 Edition,* pp. 17, 19)

6. Verse 1 reviews Paul's reason for writing this letter and refers back to a question he obviously addressed in the first letter (1 Thessalonians 4:13-5:10) regarding the coming of the Lord for believers. What was unsettling the Thessalonians (v. 2) and why?

> **Scriptural Insight:** If Paul had taught the Thessalonians that the Rapture wouldn't occur until after the terrible day of the Lord, they would not have been unsettled by the bad things happening to them. Their dismay confirms that Paul taught them the Rapture would come before God's wrath would be poured out on the earth.

To reinforce the truth he had already taught them, Paul reminded them that three things will happen when the judgments associated with the day of the Lord begin. These three "signs" are the rebellion (v. 3), the man of lawlessness being revealed (v. 3), and he who now holds him back being taken away (v. 7). This will bring about the time period called the Great Tribulation described in Daniel 9, the Gospels (Matthew 24, Mark 13, Luke 21) and Revelation. The presence of the definite article "the" with each event identifies it as unique. No other events are exactly like them. Let's look at these three signs individually, starting with the third one.

The restrainer removed

7. Read 2 Thessalonians 2:6-7. The Greek word translated "holding back" carries the idea of restraining and hindering. So we will refer to the one holding back as the restrainer.

   - The man of lawlessness is under the control of Satan (v. 9). Only something stronger than Satan could restrain him. Who is on the earth and has power stronger than Satan?

   - In what ways does the Holy Spirit presently restrain the power of lawlessness/evil in the world? See 1 Thessalonians 1:4-9; Titus 2:11-14; and other verses you know.

Think About It: It is presently as though the Holy Spirit was blocking the doorway so that Lawlessness (personified) could not enter. But at the Rapture, He will step aside, and Lawlessness will rush in … [and] overwhelm the world. (*Dr. Constable's Notes on 2 Thessalonians 2020 Edition*, p. 29)

- The Holy Spirit is active in our world through the life and work of believers. Consider what will happen when the Church is removed. How will this event affect the power of lawlessness?

Scriptural Insight: The word translated "secret" in v. 7 is actually the Greek word for "mystery." A mystery in the Bible is truth previously not revealed but now made known by God. The mystery being revealed here is [what] would follow the removal of the restrainer. … This lawless movement was already underway in Paul's day, but God was holding it back until His appointed time … God will remove the Holy Spirit [the restraining influence] from the earth in the sense that God will remove those whom He indwells, and He with them. He will not entirely abandon the earth, of course, since God is omnipresent. (*Dr. Constable's Notes on 2 Thessalonians 2020 Edition*, p. 28)

The rebellion against God

From the Greek: The Greek word translated "rebellion" in v. 3 is *apostasia*, meaning "falling away." It is where we get our English word apostasy. By definition, an apostasy is an abandoning of a position formerly held. It does not mean simply disbelieving, but it is an aggressive and positive revolt. … In the Greek Old Testament, we find it used of rebellion against God, and this becomes the accepted Biblical usage. (*Dr. Constable's Notes on 2 Thessalonians 2020 Edition*, p. 21)

Apostasy is falling away from truth that you once believed. It has been with us since the first century. And the apostles wrote about apostasy growing worse and worse through the years before the Lord comes. Apostasy is driven by people who may even call themselves "Christian" but who have not personally put their faith in Jesus Christ for their salvation. They are influential fakers who draw people away from Christ.

Remember that all genuine Christians who have trusted Christ and are indwelt by the Holy Spirit will go to be with the Lord in the Rapture so you won't be affected by this rebellion (1 Thessalonians 1:10). The unbelievers who are left behind will be enticed to join this universal rebellion against God. Perhaps the Rapture will draw some to finally put their faith in Jesus Christ and be saved, though they must live through the Tribulation.

8. Read the following verses to see what identifies such influential fakers even today and the harm they do.

   - 2 Corinthians 11:3-4, 13-15—

- 1 Timothy 4:1-2—

- 2 Timothy 4:3-4—

Think About It: What about professing Christians on the public stage (authors, worship singers, actors) who claim they no longer believe today? That seems to happen on a regular basis. Only God knows their true natures, whether believers or not. If they are true Christians, the Holy Spirit will work on their hearts to bring them back to the Lord. If they are not true Christians, they fit the descriptions you read about in the verses above.

The man of lawlessness revealed

Reading what Paul wrote in 2 Thessalonians 2:3-12 is pretty scary. This person, also known as the Antichrist in other passages, had not yet appeared when Paul wrote, nor has he appeared since that time no matter how evil some historical persons have been. How do we know that? The Rapture of the church has not taken place. The man of lawlessness will not be revealed until after that.

9. Let's look at the characteristics describing this man of lawlessness in 2 Thessalonians 2. Think of him as a counterfeit to Christ.

    - v. 4—

    - v. 9—

    - v. 10—

Think About It: Deception allows apostasy to build.. Apostasy allows the man of lawlessness to begin his rise so when the Spirit is removed, he's there ready to take the role. But we won't know who it is. And until the restrainer is removed, the Antichrist can do nothing of this magnitude.

10. The prophet Daniel spoke of this person, calling him the "ruler who will come." Read Daniel 9:24-27. What additional information do you learn?

11. ***Deeper Discoveries (optional):*** Matthew 24:1-35; Mark 13:3-34; and Luke 21:5-35 describe what will take place during the day of the Lord's judgment (the Great Tribulation) and the Second Coming of Jesus Christ to earth. These signs are not in chronological order. Remember that this occurs after the Rapture, so you will be in heaven during this time.

The Great Tribulation will be characterized by unrestrained evil. We don't need to get carried away with the Great Tribulation will be like and how very deceptively evil the Antichrist will be. But God has revealed to us some truth in 2 Thessalonians about the future of him and those who join with him in the rebellion against God.

12. What is the fate of "the man of lawlessness" according to vv. 3 and 8?

> **From the Greek:** The Lord's "coming" (v. 8, Gr. *epiphaneia*) is a different, and later event than the "gathering" (Gr. *episynagoges*) event (v. 1). The first event is the Rapture, and the second is the Second Coming. (*Dr. Constable's Notes on 2 Thessalonians 2020 Edition,* p. 30)

13. What is the destiny of all those who are deceived by the man of lawlessness and delight in wickedness (vv. 10-12)? Why is that their destiny? See also 2 Thessalonians 1:8-9 and Romans 1:18-20.

> **Focus on the Meaning:** Here is the definite judicial act of God who gives the wicked over to the evil which they have deliberately chosen." (A. T. Robertson, *Robertson's Word Pictures in the New Testament,* 2 Thessalonians 2:11)

Paul did not regard prophecy as too deep or unimportant for even new Christians. He believed prophetic truth was a vital part of the whole counsel of God, essential to victorious Christian living. He revealed what God wants us to know about our future to give us encouragement and hope and confidence in His sovereign plan for our world and all who are in it. But the day of the Lord will come unexpectedly like a thief in the night (1 Thessalonians 5:2-3). So God is the only one who knows when these things will take place. Humans can do nothing to make it happen any sooner than God chooses.

14. ***Deeper Discoveries (optional):*** Reread 2 Thessalonians 2:2. The opposite attitude toward the day of the Lord can also be taken and is prevalent today. Read 2 Peter 3:3-7. What attitude does Peter warn about? What scripture do people with this attitude have to ignore or explain away? Describe any experiences you have had with people/churches who maintain the same attitude that Peter describes. What gives them hope, if not the return of Christ?

What application will you make to gain perspective?

15. Read 2 Timothy 4:3-4 again. That describes a process by which we can become willing participants in our own deception. We can't determine the identity of "the man of lawlessness" or know the exact time of the Rapture. We can do something about apostasy in our own lives and in those within our spheres of influence.

- How do you see what Paul described taking place in our world? Do you personally know anyone like those described? How will you pray for them specifically?

- Are you careful to critically analyze what you see, read, and hear? How do you know if it is biblical truth or not?

16. Consider those professing Christians on the public stage (authors, worship singers, actors) who claim they no longer believe today. These modern-day influencers are often praised in social media for having the courage to publicly express their doubts and renounce their faith/belief system. How can we as believers respond to this in such a way as to promote honest discussion about their doubts while continuing to stand firm in the truth of God's Word?

Respond to the Lord about what you learned today.

DAY THREE STUDY

Read 2 Thessalonians 2:1-17. Ask the Lord Jesus to teach you through His Word.

What does it mean?

Today, we will focus on vv. 13-17.

17. In contrast to the lawless unbelievers just referenced in v. 12, Paul was grateful that he could "always thank God" for the Thessalonians. He confirmed again who they are in the mind of God. Note: "Firstfruits" refers to the first part of a harvest offered to God. The harvest began at Pentecost and continues until Jesus returns.

    What did Paul say about the Thessalonians believers in v. 13?

> **Focus on the Meaning:** The word translated "loved by the Lord" is the same word used when God said about Jesus, "You are my Son, whom I love" in Mark 1:11; 9:7. You are loved that much! Also, the word translated "chosen" meant to lift up, to move something toward the sun. We are definitely lifted up by our God, aren't we?

18. God called them through the gospel so they might share in "the glory of our Lord Jesus Christ" (v. 14). Read John 17:10, 22, 24 and 2 Thessalonians 1:12. What do you learn that helps you to understand sharing in His glory?

19. Because of being chosen, sanctified, and destined for a future share in Christ's glory,

    - What should we as believers continue to do now (v. 15)?

    - What does it mean to "hold fast to the teachings we passed on to you?" To what teachings was Paul referring? Refer back to 1 Thessalonians 2:13; 4:8.

Focus on the Meaning: Inspired tradition, in Paul's sense, is not a supplementary oral tradition completing *our* written Word, but it is identical with the written Word *now* complete... [since] the death of St. John, the last apostle. (*Dr. Constable's Notes on 2 Thessalonians 2020 Edition*, p. 36)

20. Looking at vv. 16-17: Paul wrote out what he was praying for the Thessalonians throughout both of his letters.

    • This time, Paul asked God for what?

    • How would knowing what he prayed for them add to their encouragement to stand firm?

    • Although God is the Ultimate Encourager, whom does He often use? See 1 Thessalonians 3:2, 6-9 and any other verses you can add.

    Focus on the Meaning: Paul addressed his prayer to the Lord Jesus Christ as well as to God the Father (also 1 Thessalonians 3:11). It's okay to address prayer to Jesus. The Father, the Son, and the Holy Spirit are equally God, equally powerful, and equally involved in answering our prayer (Romans 8:26-27; 34).

What application will you make to gain perspective?

21. We are blessed and instructed as we read Paul's written prayers in the New Testament letters that he wrote under the Holy Spirit's inspiration. When you correspond with someone who is going through a tough time, do you write out your specific prayer for them in your emails, texts, or on social media? Why or why not? Consider beginning this practice today and watch what God does through that encouragement.

22. Considering this whole chapter, the wrath of God's judgment displayed in "the day of the Lord" sounds awful. But our God has given us "good hope" (v. 16). How does knowing that you will be gathered up with Christ in the Rapture and not experience the awfulness of the day of the Lord give you comfort, hope, and keep you from *giving way to fear?* Can you trust Him to carry out His plans and still take care of you?

Praise God for His great salvation for you and me who have chosen to love the truth and believe His gospel!

Pray 2 Thessalonians 2:16-17 for yourself and others.

Recommended: Listen to the podcast "Gain More Perspective about the Great Tribulation" after doing this lesson to reinforce what you have learned. Use the listener guide on the next page.

Gain More Perspective about the Great Tribulation

THE EXPECTATION

- The Jews of Jesus' day expected that when the Messiah comes, God would begin a new age—His kingdom—first by resurrecting and judging all the dead, then giving the Holy Spirit to the righteous, and finally righting all the wrongs on planet Earth. The Messiah would reign as king over the whole earth from Jerusalem. They just didn't know that God's plan would be a two-stage process.

- When the early Christians spoke of Jesus being raised from the dead, they were claiming that something happened to Jesus, which had never happened to anyone else—yet. The resurrection declared that what Jesus did in His life and in His death was the work of God's son—the Messiah (Romans 1:2-4). Because of Jesus' finished work on the cross, God could give His Spirit to faithful believers. If you want to understand that better, I suggest you listen to the Series 12 podcasts about the Gospel as God's cure for our fatal sin disease.

- What the Jews expected was their best guess. Jesus fulfilled the first part and promised to come back to finish the job and restore everything. *Acts 3:20-21*

- Until the time comes for God to restore everything, there's waiting involved. This UNTIL time is also called the "time of the Gentiles" in Scripture.

- On earth, the Rapture of the believers is the signal that the time of God's grace to the Gentiles ends. Judgment of all the nations happens during a period of 7 years called "The Great Tribulation." Most of the book of Revelation covers this time period. But we also see references to it in 2 Thessalonians chapter 2. It sounds awful!

THE DAY OF THE LORD HASN'T HAPPENED YET

- Paul wrote so confidently in 2 Thessalonians chapter 2 that the three signs declaring the day of the Lord was here had not happened yet. The restrainer of evil had not been removed. The man of lawlessness had not been revealed. And the religious rebellion had not occurred. That is still true today. The day of the Lord hasn't happened yet.

- The Tribulation is a time when God takes His hands off and lets those who reject Him enjoy the fruit of their decision. He gives them over to the wickedness that they want to do. He allows sinful people to experience the sinful behaviors that they want to enjoy. *Romans 1; 1 Timothy 4:1-2*

- The wickedness we see now will get much worse during the Tribulation, enhanced by the revealing of the man of lawlessness. He will be a counterfeit Christ who serves the lies that humans want to believe about not needing God. *2 Thessalonians 2:10-12*

- Humans make the choice against God—to not believe the truth and to delight in wickedness. God doesn't make that choice for them. But for everyone who digs in their heels and refuses God, He declares them guilty of punishment. He lets them have what they want—life apart from Him and His goodness.

- Yet, He continues to offer eternal life to anyone who repents of their sin and trusts in Him, even during the Great Tribulation. That's God's grace and mercy.

TRUTH FOR NOW

Here are some things we can know for sure:

- *What We Can Know for Sure:* Jesus is coming back to gather His own, and not one believer is going to miss it. We just don't know when He is returning.

- *What We Can Know for Sure:* Jesus said conditions on this planet are not going to get better but worse! We can forget the whole idea of world peace until He comes back. Although believers are encouraged to individually live in peace with each other and with unbelievers, we humans can never bring about world peace. *Mark 13:7-8*

- *What We Can Know for Sure:* Jesus described a great time of worldwide, massive tribulation. This Great Tribulation hasn't happened yet. *Mark 13:14-23*

- *What We Can Know for Sure:* Jesus is returning to planet Earth with His angels to defeat the evil forces against Him and set up His Kingdom in Jerusalem. *Revelation 19-20*

FOR NOW, WATCH OUT THAT NO ONE DECEIVES YOU.

- To them and to all of us, Jesus says, "Stay alert." In Mark chapter 13, Jesus warned His disciples 8 times to "watch out," "be on guard," and "stay alert." A Christ-follower's greatest danger is not war, not calamity, not suffering, not persecution, and not even betrayal. It is deception. *Mark 13:5*

- Deception feeds apostasy—an aggressive and positive revolt against God by so-called religious people. Apostasy is driven by people who may even call themselves "Christian" but are influential fakers who draw people away from Christ, especially when they claim to no longer believe in Him. *2 Corinthians 11:3*

- We have a spiritual enemy, and deceiving us is one of his best means for making us ineffective at pursuing Christ completely.

- Don't let other people's thoughts be a replacement for the Bible or your dependence on Christ. Compare what you are being told with what God's Word says. *2 Thessalonians 2:15*

Let Jesus satisfy your heart with His perspective on life in the present and in the future. Then, live securely in Him during this time of waiting.

11: Perspective on Life in the Waiting

2 Thessalonians 3:1-18

DAY ONE STUDY—GET THE BIG PICTURE

Ask the Lord Jesus to teach you through His Word.

What does the Bible say?

Read the Bible passage below (NIV) including verses from the last lesson. Use your own method (colored pencils, lines, shapes) to mark 1) anything that grabs your attention, 2) words you want to understand, and 3) topics you have seen before in this letter. Draw arrows between thoughts that connect.

2 *[13] But we ought always to thank God for you, brothers and sisters loved by the Lord, because God chose you as firstfruits to be saved through the sanctifying work of the Spirit and through belief in the truth. [14] He called you to this through our gospel, that you might share in the glory of our Lord Jesus Christ. [15] So then, brothers and sisters, stand firm and hold fast to the teachings we passed on to you, whether by word of mouth or by letter. [16] May our Lord Jesus Christ himself and God our Father, who loved us and by his grace gave us eternal encouragement and good hope, [17] encourage your hearts and strengthen you in every good deed and word.*

3 *[1] As for other matters, brothers and sisters, pray for us that the message of the Lord may spread rapidly and be honored, just as it was with you. [2] And pray that we may be delivered from wicked and evil people, for not everyone has faith. [3] But the Lord is faithful, and he will strengthen you and protect you from the evil one. [4] We have confidence in the Lord that you are doing and will continue to do the things we command. [5] May the Lord direct your hearts into God's love and Christ's perseverance.*

[6] In the name of the Lord Jesus Christ, we command you, brothers and sisters, to keep away from every believer who is idle and disruptive and does not live according to the teaching you received from us. [7] For you yourselves know how you ought to follow our example. We were not idle when we were with you, [8] nor did we eat anyone's food without paying for it. On the contrary, we worked night and day, laboring and toiling so that we would not be a burden to any of you. [9] We did this, not because we do not have the right to such help, but in order to offer ourselves as a model for you to imitate. [10] For even when we were with you, we gave you this rule: "The one who is unwilling to work shall not eat."

[11] We hear that some among you are idle and disruptive. They are not busy; they are busybodies. [12] Such people we command and urge in the Lord Jesus Christ to settle down and earn the food they eat. [13] And as for you, brothers and sisters, never tire of doing what is good.

[14] Take special note of anyone who does not obey our instruction in this letter. Do not associate with them, in order that they may feel ashamed. [15] Yet do not regard them as an enemy, but warn them as you would a fellow believer.

[16] Now may the Lord of peace himself give you peace at all times and in every way. The Lord be with all of you. [17] I, Paul, write this greeting in my own hand, which is the distinguishing mark in all my letters. This is how I write. [18] The grace of our Lord Jesus Christ be with you all.

1. What grabbed your attention from these verses?

2. What verses or specific words do you want to understand better?

3. What words or phrases are repeated in this passage? Give verses.

4. What topics (if any) in this passage have we previously studied in 1 or 2 Thessalonians?

5. *Gain perspective:* From this lesson's passage (3:1-18), choose one verse to dwell upon all week long. Write it in the space below. Ask God to teach you through this verse.

Respond to the Lord about what you learned today.

DAY TWO STUDY

Read 2 Thessalonians 3:1-18. Ask the Lord Jesus to teach you through His Word.

What does it mean?

Today, we will focus on vv. 1-5.

6. In 1 Thessalonians 5:25, Paul had asked them to pray for him and his co-workers. Read 1 Thessalonians 2:18; 3:7,10,11. For what did he need the Thessalonians to pray for him?

7. In 2 Thessalonians 3:1-2, Paul asked them to pray for him. What prayer needs did he share with them?

> **Focus on the Meaning:** Notice the two parts of his prayer. First comes the spreading of the message as we have seen in 1 Thessalonians 1:5,8 and 2:2. The second part is for people to receive the message. See 1 Thessalonians 1:6 and 2:13.

8. Ten years after writing 2 Thessalonians, Paul was confined in a Roman house and chained to a Roman soldier. Read Colossians 4:3-4. After all those years of preaching the gospel and establishing churches, what do these verses reflect about his heart and humility?

9. In 2 Thessalonians 3:2, the word "delivered" means *rescued, away from*. Paul was in Corinth writing this letter.

    • Read Acts 18:5-17. What was happening there?

    • Assuming the Thessalonians prayed for him, how did God answer their prayer?

10. God used both personal assurance to Paul through His Word as well as a government official who was not even a Christian.

- We have His word with us in our Bible. What does the Holy Spirit do with that to deliver us from our fear? See also John 16:13 and 1 Corinthians 2:10-13.

- We have governmental authorities. Read Romans 13:1-4 and 1 Timothy 2:1-4. How does God use authorities to benefit His people?

> **Scriptural Insight:** Regarding authorities commending those who do right and punishing those who do wrong, Paul is not stating that this will always be true but is describing the proper, ideal function of rulers. When civil rulers overstep their proper function, the Christian is to obey God rather than man (see Acts 4:19; 5:29). (*NIV Study Bible*, note on Romans 13:3, p. 1726)

11. Looking at 2 Thessalonians 3:3-4:

- What does it mean that God is faithful? Faithful to whom? To do what? See also 1 Thessalonians 5:23-24 and Philippians 1:6; 2:13.

- How did knowing that God is faithful give Paul confidence that the Thessalonians would mature in their faith? See 2 Thessalonians 1:3-4.

> **Scriptural Insight:** The character of God should be the basis for a Christian's confidence. Because God has promised to supply believers' needs, Paul could rest in the assurance that He would provide strength to withstand temptation and trials, and protection from the adversary and his emissaries. (*The Bible Knowledge Commentary New Testament*, p. 722)

12. Read 2 Thessalonians 3:5 again. Paul is about to exhort the church to discipline some of their own (vv. 6-15). How would having God's love (for God and for others) and Christ's perseverance help them to be obedient to the Lord's commands and address the problems in the church?

What application will you make to gain perspective?

13. Are you confident in God? Do you know without a shadow of a doubt, that He who is faithful, will always be there for you? Explain your answer and how this gives you encouragement in your own prayer life.

14. Respond to the Lord about what you learned today by adapting the words from 2 Thessalonians 3:1-5 into a prayer for yourself. Then, say those words to the Lord, expecting Him to answer because those are within His will for you.

DAY THREE STUDY

Read 2 Thessalonians 3:1-18. Ask the Lord Jesus to teach you through His Word.

What does it mean?

First, we will focus on vv. 6-15.

> **From the Greek:** The description "idle and disruptive" translates a Greek word meaning "disorderly, out of ranks (as for a soldier), deviating from the prescribed rule of order." It is someone who is unruly ("disorderly and disruptive and not amenable to discipline or control") who is affecting the lives of others. The Greek word translated "busybody" means "to bustle about uselessly, to busy one's self about trifling, needless, useless matters." This is a problem to which idleness often leads.

Idleness must have been a common problem in Thessalonica as Paul mentions it several times (1 Thessalonians 4:11-12; 5:14). Review what you learned in Lesson 6 Day Three Study.

15. Look at vv. 6 and 11.

- Paul says to stay away from whom?

- Why is being a busybody rather than a busy worker not good?

> **Scriptural Insight:** The proper management of one's home and family is considered to be work (2 Timothy 5:11-14).

16. In what ways does an idle and disruptive person affect...?

- Herself—

- Others around her (family, neighbors, co-workers)—

- An entire organization—

> **Focus on the Meaning:** The word translated "keep away" means to diminish contact, remove oneself, withdraw, or abstain from familiar interaction. Paul's rebuke is to those who **would not** work, not those who could not work. This is a very important difference. God's Word gives many ways to help those who are poor or unable to work.

17. What is Paul's rebuke and command to those who are idle and disruptive busybodies (vv. 12-13)?

> **From the Greek:** The Greek word translated "settle down (NIV)" or "work quietly (ESV)" in verse 12 points to the quality of mind that is to be associated with their working. It denotes a condition of inward peace and tranquility reflecting itself in outward calmness. It is the opposite of their fussy activity as busybodies.

18. Discuss Paul's advice to the church members who are not idle and disruptive—what to do and why (vv. 6, 14-15). See 1 Corinthians 5:9-13 and 2 Corinthians 2:5-7 for a similar situation.

Scriptural Insight: The faithful majority in the church was to separate, probably individually and socially, from the unruly to alert the offenders to the fact that their behavior was not acceptable. The desired result was that they would repent. Paul had earlier warned those who were idle (1 Thess. 5:14), but evidently, they had not responded. Now firmer measures were necessary (cf. Matt. 18:15-17). The offenders constituted a minority who lived undisciplined lives contrary to the teaching and example of the missionaries. (*Dr. Constable's Notes on 2 Thessalonians 2020 Edition,* pp. 40-41)

19. Paul and his team could have expected to be paid for their teaching but chose not to do so. From 2 Thessalonians 3:7-10, what example did Paul and his companions set as the proper attitude toward work? See also 1 Thessalonians 2:9.

Think About It: Don't get alarmed by the phrase "day and night." Remember that Paul and his team were single men who considered the Thessalonians to be their family. They were not neglecting their family just to earn more money (greed) or to gain prestige for themselves (pleasing men, 1 Thessalonians 2:4-6). In everything, they aimed to please God.

20. Work is good. God is a worker, and He has designed us to be purposeful with our time, energy, and skills. We are co-workers with Him (Psalm 8:4-6; Ephesians 2:10; and 2 Thessalonians 1:11). Read Colossians 3:22-24 and Ephesians 6:5-9. Although slavery is always wrong, these verses relate to all work that you do.

- How are believers to do any work?

- What would that look like in your life regarding all work that you do regardless of where?

21. Why should Christians make the best employees? See also 1 Thessalonians 4:1,11-12.

22. **Deeper Discoveries (optional):** One of the many benefits of work is provision for yourself and your family. Another benefit is having enough to share with others. Read Galatians 6:7-10; 2 Corinthians 9:10-15; and 1 Timothy 6:18-19. What do you learn?

23. Read 2 Thessalonians 3:16-18 again. For what can we pray and why?

Paul's ending to this letter included words he penned himself so his letters could be distinguished as authentic. See also 1 Corinthians 16:21; Galatians 6:11; and Colossians 4:18. This avoided the problem of forgeries, as in 2 Thessalonians 2:2. The church leaders knew for sure which ones were definitely from him. This should give you confidence that these letters you've studied were written by Paul as declared in the salutations.

What application will you make to gain perspective?

24. Is there an idle and disruptive person affecting your life? Are you the idle and disruptive person affecting your life? How will you apply what you have learned in this lesson?

25. Considering yourself as a worker:

   • Whether your employer is a business or your home, in what practical ways can you commit to working hard?

   • How has your work ethic already benefited you and others around you? Are you inspiring those in your sphere of influence to have an excellent work ethic?

26. How has this study of 1 and 2 Thessalonians changed or sharpened your perspective about life in the future and life in the waiting "until" Jesus appears?

Historical Insight: What happened to the church? Ancient Thessalonica is known today by its original name, Thessaloniki. In the middle of the second century, the Emperor Antoninus Pius wrote to the people of Thessalonica, telling them to take no new steps against the Christians, implying the church was still active. At the beginning of the third century, Tertullian couples it with Philippi as a church where the original letters of the Apostles are still being read. For centuries, the city remained one of the chief strongholds of Christianity, and it won for itself the title of "the Orthodox City," not only by the tenacity and vigor of its resistance to the successive attacks of various barbarous races, but also by being largely responsible for their conversion to Christianity. Modern Thessaloniki is second only to Athens in population. During World War I, it served as an important Allied base. In World War II, it was captured by the German army, and the large Jewish population was deported. At present, only a minority of the inhabitants are Christians. The modern city is rich in examples of Byzantine ecclesiastical architecture and art, and possesses 12 churches and 25 synagogues. The memory of the Apostle Paul is apparently still honored by the inhabitants. Several mission organizations are active in planting and/or supporting churches in Thessaloniki.

Pray 2 Thessalonians 3:16 for yourself and others who need His peace.

Recommended: Listen to the podcast "Gain the Biblical Perspective on Work Until He Comes" after doing this lesson to reinforce what you have learned. Use the listener guide on the next page.

Gain the Biblical Perspective on Work Until He Comes

We humans love figuring out mysteries. Prophecy is the biggest mystery ever. God alone knows how the puzzle pieces fit together inside the signs He gave us that the time was finally here.

One of the by-products of an excessive interest in prophecy is idleness when it comes to doing the work of the Lord today. Sitting around just waiting for Jesus' appearing is not pleasing to God. That seemed to be happening in Thessalonica. And it happens today.

Since Paul talks a lot about working in 2 Thessalonians chapter 3, we can focus on Christ's purpose for you in your workplace during this time of waiting for Him to come and gather His own.

CHRIST'S PURPOSE FOR YOU IN YOUR WORKPLACE

- Work in any culture is…well, work. Sometimes enjoyable. Often hard and exhausting. Sometimes challenging because of the people with whom you work rather than the work itself. That can apply to any kind of work—inside or outside of your home. When you're working with your God-given skills, all work can be an act of worship.

  *Whatever you do, work at it with all your heart, as **working for the Lord**, not for human masters, since you know that you will receive an inheritance from the Lord as a reward. It **is the Lord Christ you are serving**. (Colossians 3:23-24)*

- Your workplace (be it home, office, factory floor, school room, or road construction) is your mission field. Your work environment is where you must intentionally practice letting Jesus live His life through you—in difficult situations, with challenging people, and with integrity that honors the Lord Jesus Christ..

A FEW TRUTHS ABOUT ANY KIND OF WORK

- **Truth #1: Work is God's idea.** God is a worker. God created work in the beginning before sin ever entered into His world. Work is good. Sin corrupted work so it got a lot harder to do. Then, Jesus came along to renew us and restore our approach to work as He lives in us and through us. We are free to work for God's glory now.

- **Truth #2: Work is an avenue for accomplishing God's mission.** When Jesus commissioned His followers to make disciples everywhere they went, none of them were on church staff or in mission organizations. They were ordinary people going to work every day. In the same way, we are Jesus' ambassadors at work—in the conference room, on the factory floor, at the lunch break, on the playground, and in the kitchen. As we do our work with integrity and intentionally build relationships with our coworkers, clients or family members, Jesus is actively involved in that. Work is your mission field and your platform to let Christ live His life through you.

- **Truth #3: Work is the place where God grows us into maturity.** The Spirit of God uses our relationships, successes, failures, and experiences at work as tools in our spiritual growth. He teaches us to have the mind of Christ at work, to treat people as Jesus did, and to grow in our jobs under His guidance. God uses our work to mature us.

- **Truth #4: Work has purpose beyond ourselves.** God designed work for the good of the world—not just for ourselves. Our work impacts the people in our work environment, our clients, and our managers. Work provides jobs, fuels the economy, and allows culture to flourish. When we work, we can taste the goodness of God intended for work in the beginning.

- **Truth #5: Work is where we practice depending on Jesus more than on ourselves.** In Colossians 3:17, we are reminded to do everything we say or do in light of Jesus as Lord.

- **Truth #6: Work can become an addiction that takes the focus off of Christ and puts it on yourself instead.** You know that you have let work become an addiction when you are obsessively thinking about freeing up more time for your work. When you develop health problems because of work-related stress and overwork, that's not working for the Lord. Another clue is when you use your work to maintain your self-worth. The modern term for that is workism. Workism is the belief that your work is the center of your identity. For a Christian, your work is never the center of your identity. Christ is. So if you recognize this in yourself, go to the Lord and ask Him to free you from the addiction. Talk to a counsellor about this as well.

A FEW QUESTIONS ABOUT FAITH IN THE WORKPLACE

- *How do you live out your faith in your workplace?* As I mentioned before, you do that by being the person described in most of 1 Thessalonians chapter 5. That's recognizing Jesus Christ as Lord of your life and your behavior. Let Him live His life through you to invite others around you to want to know Him. Ask Jesus to help you do that and trust Him to work in you and through you.

- *What is legal to do at work?* Go to firstliberty.org to find out what is legal for a Christian to do in any workplace. That's firstliberty.org. You might be surprised by what you can legally do to live out your faith in the marketplace. And be grateful.

- *How do you invest in your co-workers without stealing time from your employer?* You use whatever break time or interaction opportunities you have available to get to know your co-workers and minister to them. Ask Jesus to help you be creative and caring. I have several Bible Studies that are short and easy and would fit nicely in a lunch hour time frame.

- *What if you hate what you do for work?* That's where you submit yourself to Jesus Christ as Lord over you and even over that job. Let Him teach you how to be thankful for that work or lead you to something else. Whatever He brings into your life that makes you more dependent upon Him is good for you. Work is a great environment to learn that.

Remember this. Your work belongs to Jesus. He will enable you to find purpose in it that brings glory to Him. So keep working diligently, producing what is needed, providing for yourself and others, and preparing the way for others to see Christ in you.

Let Jesus satisfy your heart with His perspective on life in the present and in the future. Then, live securely in Him during this time of waiting.

Extra Lesson: The Rest of the Story

Revelation 19-22

This is the rest of the story to what we have covered in 1 and 2 Thessalonians.

Trying to understand all the prophecies about the end times is like having a bunch of puzzle pieces that look similar but without the picture on the box top to tell you how to arrange them. All we know for sure are the border pieces. We can put the 4 sides of the puzzle together. Those are events we know will definitely happen. Those 4 sides are (1) Jesus' appearing for the Rapture of believers, (2) the Great Tribulation that follows, (3) the revealing of the Antichrist during the Tribulation, and (4) Christ coming to exact justice against unbelievers and setting up His kingdom on earth. We don't know when or how the rest of the pieces fit inside the border. But God gives us a glimpse of what it will be like after He puts those inside puzzle pieces together.

DAY ONE STUDY

Ask the Lord Jesus to teach you through His Word.

What does it mean?

> **Scriptural Insight:** The climactic theme of both the Old Testament and the New Testament is the promise of the coming of the Messiah to set things right.

1. Read Acts 3:19-21. What did Peter assure believers about the future?

> **From the Greek:** The Greek word translated "restore" or restoration" in Acts 3:21 comes from *apo* (back, again) and *kathistemi* (to set in order). It is used of the restoration of estates to rightful owners. (*Vines Expository Dictionary of Old and New Testament Words*, p. 530)

2. Read 2 Peter 3:1-13.

> **Scriptural Insight:** "The day of the Lord" refers to a future time in which God will be more directly and dramatically involved in world affairs than He has been since the earthly ministry of the Lord Jesus Christ. That day begins immediately after the Rapture of the church, includes the Lord's judgment against sin (Revelation 6-18), and ends with the conclusion of the Millennial Kingdom (Revelation 20). In the New Testament, the phrase "the last days" for Christians refers to that time period between Christ's ascension and His appearing to gather His own (at the Rapture).

- In vv. 3-9, what attitudes will characterize the last days, particularly that of the scoffers?

- How have you seen this prophecy fulfilled in the past 100 years?

- In vv. 10-13, what information is given about the future?

3. Why will God recreate (or renew, as some translations say) the current heavens ("space," which we call the universe) and earth? See also Romans 8:19-22.

> **Focus on the Meaning:** Scholars disagree on whether the earth and heavens are totally recreated in perfect newness or just purged of all sin and corruption so that they are new again (renewed). Since this is in the mind and hands of God, we don't need to speculate about what He does. We can look at the purpose and result as part of our glorious future. And we can praise Him for the promise of life in a world that is totally free of sin and its corruption.

4. *Gain perspective:* Considering all that you have learned in this study of 1 and 2 Thessalonians, why should the study of prophecy regarding God's future plans for the earth NOT cause you fear but give you hope instead?

Respond to the Lord about what you learned today.

DAY TWO STUDY

Ask the Lord Jesus to teach you through His Word.

What does it mean?

> *The secret things belong to the Lord our God, but **the things revealed belong to us** and to our children forever ... (Deuteronomy 29:29)*

Let's consider a possible timetable for the end. No one knows for sure what will happen and when. But we can make our best guesses based on what is revealed in the Bible. So the visual below (source unknown) is a best guess.

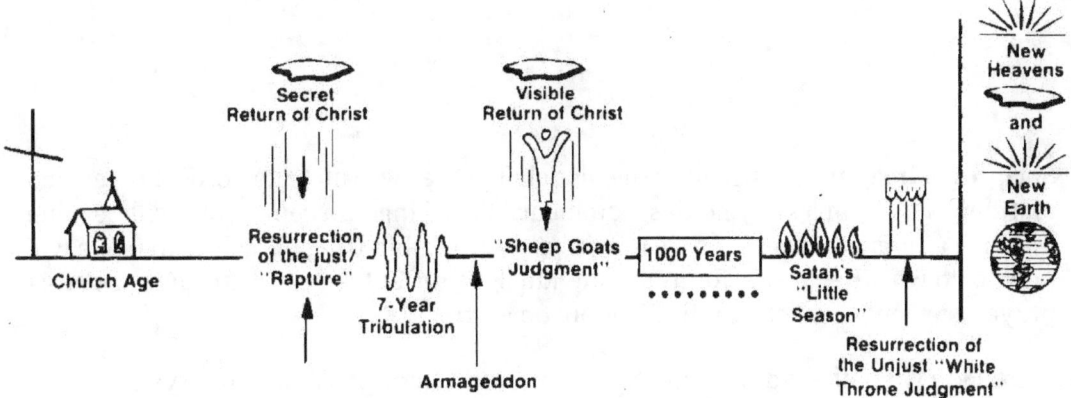

As Paul wrote in 1 Thessalonians 4:13-17, believers (living and those who have already died) will be "raptured" or "caught up" to meet Christ in the air when the time comes that God has predetermined. Then all believers will go to heaven to be with Christ in new glorified, heavenly bodies. Based on what we learned in 1 and 2 Thessalonians, a time of Great Tribulation will follow the Rapture of believers. The books of Daniel and Revelation also describe this 7-year period of tribulation as a time of extreme deception, wars, and suffering.

At the end of the 7-year period, Christ will gloriously return to earth as He promised (Revelation 19), setting up His kingdom on earth. Revelation 20 says this kingdom will last 1000 years. A thousand years is called a millennium. So His kingdom is called the Millennial Kingdom. Those believers who died during the Tribulation period will be given resurrection bodies and, along with the raptured believers, will rule with Christ on the earth in their glorified bodies.

Those earthly humans who trusted in Christ during the Tribulation and are still alive will live on past the battle of Armageddon described in Revelation chapter 19. They will remain on Earth to enter the millennial kingdom in their natural, mortal bodies. These are the ones who will produce children during the millennial kingdom, not those in glorified bodies (Mark 12:24-25).

5. Read Revelation 19:11-21. This describes Jesus' triumphant victory over Satan and his cohorts at the end of the Tribulation. This is the Second Coming referenced in 2 Thessalonians 1:7-9; 2 Thessalonians 2:8; and Luke 21:27.

6. When Jesus returns to Earth, He will bring His kingdom with Him. Read the following verses. What information is given about Christ's reign as king on earth?

   • Revelation 20:1-6—

   • Isaiah 9:6-7—

   Scriptural Insight: Jesus gave us the model of prayer we call "The Lord's Prayer" in Matthew 6:9-13. In it, we find this statement, "Your kingdom come, your will be done, on earth as it is in heaven." As we pray this, we are submitting ourselves to God's will now to do what He desires for us as individuals to do. But the ultimate answer to this prayer is when Jesus sets up His kingdom on earth.

7. All of creation was affected by sin entering the world through Adam and Eve.

   • Read Genesis 1:29-31—this is *Paradise* at the beginning.

   • Read Genesis 3:17-19; 9:1-3; and Romans 8:19-22—this is *Paradise Lost*.

8. Now read the following verses that give a glimpse of *Paradise Regained* in the future. What is being restored during the millennial reign of Christ as described in Isaiah?

   • Isaiah 11:1-10—

   • Isaiah 65:20-25—

Scriptural Insight: Often in the Old Testament, references to the first coming of Christ and the second coming of Christ are found in the same paragraph, sometimes in the same verse. Only when we are able to separate out what happened at His first coming can we see what is still ahead for us at His second coming.

9. All of the nations were affected by the confusion of languages at the Tower of Babel. We have seen how God restored a oneness to believers representing all nations at Pentecost through the indwelling Holy Spirit who makes all believers part of one Body—the Body of Christ. Read the following verses to see what God will restore to all people in the future millennial reign.

  - Zephaniah 3:9—

  - Zechariah 14:9—

  - Revelation 5:6-10—

Think About It: Nations will still form, including Israel. It is a big planet. God is a God of order. Every language will have "Jesus" only as God. The nations will be one again in spirit and cooperation—united in serving God.

10. Read Revelation 20:7-15. Jesus has all authority over heaven and earth right now. He will one day exercise that authority when He physically rules as king on planet Earth. Evil will no longer have free reign on earth. But mortal human life will continue. What happens at the end of the 1000 years according to verses 7-10?

Focus on the Meaning: Mortal humans will still have the freedom of choice that God originally gave Adam and Eve. That means they will still have the sin nature, what the Bible calls the flesh. Since Satan and his demons are bound up for the whole 1000 years, they cannot deceive anyone. If anyone chooses to rebel against the king, it's because of his/her own lusts. No one can blame the world or the devil. And justice will be swift. But after Satan is released, those with rebellious hearts will join him.

Even with the perfect, righteous King Jesus ruling all of the earth, visible to everyone, mortal humans will choose to rebel against Him. Does that surprise you or not?

What application will you make to gain perspective?

11. Jesus told His disciples in Matthew 6:10 that we should pray for His kingdom to come and God's will to be done on earth as it is in heaven. That will happen and you, dear Christian, will be in your glorified body back on earth, doing whatever work Jesus gives to you. From everything you have learned in this day's study, picture daily life in your community under Jesus' reign compared to what it is today. It's okay to take what is revealed in the Scriptures about the Kingdom and consider what it might be like to live there daily. What might be the same? What might be different?

Respond to the Lord about what you learned today.

DAY THREE STUDY

Ask the Lord Jesus to teach you through His Word.

What does it mean?

From Revelation 20, we learn that Satan will be bound for 1000 years as Christ reigns on the earth. Worship will center in Jerusalem. There will be worldwide peace between people and even among animals. Earth will be filled with the knowledge of the Lord. But not all will believe in Christ even then because the sin nature has not been removed from mortal humans born during this time. At the end of the 1000 years, Satan will be freed and will lead unbelievers against Christ. But Christ will defeat Satan and his followers permanently. God will also do something to heaven and earth so they are both restored to newness. We are confident there is a heaven wherever God is—both now and in the future.

12. Read Revelation 21:1-8. Have you ever wanted to throw out all your clothes and go shopping, and get everything new? Well, God does just that.

- What does God declare in v. 5?

- From vv. 1-4, write down all that is declared in these four verses.

Looking at v. 1, some think the word "seas" is referring to inland seas between land areas like the Mediterranean Sea, not the oceans in total. This might also refer to the land areas brought together into one continent again as it was at creation.

> **Scriptural Insight:** There is a glorious future awaiting the redeemed. The current earth and heavens (universe) will be "delivered from the bondage of corruption into ... glorious liberty" (Romans 8:21). God will make them all new again, with all the scars of sin and death burned away by His refining fires. The explicit references in the Bible to these "renewed" heavens and earth assure us that they will be so wonderful that this present earth and its heavens will soon be altogether forgotten. Not only will no sin be present there, neither will the results of sin and the curse. It is this new earth (that is, the earth made new) which will then continue forever. This is where you as a believer will spend eternity.

13. Read Revelation 21:9-27. What are some of the characteristics of the New Jerusalem?

    • Vv. 9-21—

    • Vv. 22-27—

> **Scriptural Insight:** From Revelation 21:23 and 22:5, we are told that God's light will be enough to give light to the New Jerusalem (all 1400 cubic miles of it). This is similar to what He did at the beginning of creation in Genesis 1:3.

14. Read Revelation 22:1-21. Reference is made to the Tree of Life in this chapter.

> **Scriptural Insight:** Both the "tree of life" in Eden, and the "tree of life" in the New Jerusalem (Rev. 22:2, 14, 19), are presented as literal trees. (*Dr. Constable's Notes on Revelation 2020 Edition*, p. 48)

    • What will be flowing from the throne of God (vv. 1-2)? See also Joel 3:18 for a description of the flowing water and Genesis 2:10 regarding Eden.

- In Revelation 22:2-3, 14, and 19, what new information is given about the Tree of Life?

- How does this information help you understand the role of the Tree of Life in Eden (Genesis 2:9; 3:22-24)?

From the Greek: The Greek word translated "healing" or "therapy" (*therapeian*) is similar to a word translated elsewhere as "household" (Matthew 24:45; Luke 12:42). In such cases, "therapy" refers to a staff of servants employed in keeping the affairs of a great house running efficiently. Therapy could mean effective service of the nations (verse 3) that include all the believers since Creation from all over the earth. It could also be translated as "health-giving." Since there is no sickness in heaven, the tree's fruit and leaves could also contribute to the physical or emotional well-being of everyone.

What application will you make to gain perspective?

15. Imagine what it will be like for you to live there in the city with God as well as going forth from the city to places on the new earth. God gives us the description so it is okay. In fact, He wants us to think about that glorious place which will be our future home! Feel free to use any creative means (poem, song, drawing, prayer) to express your gratitude and joy. **"Everything old is new again"—restoration complete! Praise God for His future plans for you!**

16. ***Deeper Discoveries (optional):*** Read Randy Alcorn's book *Heaven* or any other good resource on what life will be like in the new heavens and earth

Recommended: Listen to the podcast "Heaven on Earth" after doing this lesson to reinforce what you have learned. Use the listener guide on the next page.

Heaven on Earth

The LORD reigns! Let the earth be happy! Let the many coastlands rejoice! (Psalm 97:1)

On earth, the Rapture of the believers is a signal that the time of the Gentiles has ended. The Great Tribulation begins. Most of the book of Revelation describes what happens then. Many Jews will believe during the Tribulation as well as some Gentiles. Revelation chapter 19 describes what will happen at the end of the 7 years of Tribulation. Jesus will return to earth. He'll fight the enemies on earth, defeat them, and set up His kingdom prophesied so much in both the Old and New Testaments.

THE KINGDOM BEGINS ON EARTH

- Based upon an understanding of Scripture, when Jesus returns to set up His Kingdom (Revelation 20), He will be bringing His people with Him. We will be coming with Him for the battle where He defeats the Antichrist and all who are fighting with Him against God. Victory is assured. Jesus will win!

- King Jesus will be king over all. Jerusalem will be His capital. Nations will still form, including Israel. Revelation 20 says this kingdom will last 1000 years. A thousand years is called a millenium. So His kingdom is called the Millenial Kingdom. Isaiah is filled with descriptions of the Millenial Kingdom, especially chapters 11 and 65. Every Christian who had died on earth or been raptured will be returning with Jesus and will be staying on to serve Him in His Kingdom.

- Those earthly humans who trusted in Christ during the Tribulation will live on past the battle of Armageddon described in Revelation chapter 19. They will be mortal humans dealing with the whole change of rulers. All the new rulers will always do the right thing.

KING JESUS WILL REIGN OVER A PARTIALLY RESTORED EARTH.

- King Jesus will reign over an earth that is partially restored to its original created state.

  - ✓ Isaiah tells us that animals will revert back to being vegetarian. Animals and people will not fear one another so there will be no fierce, violent, and dangerous creatures.
  - ✓ Future millennials will marry and have babies. They will live to be well over 100 years again. Never will a baby or child die. Only the wicked will die early.
  - ✓ People will build houses, plant crops, and eat well. They will work and enjoy the benefits. Work will be a pleasure.
  - ✓ Needs will be addressed immediately because God says in Isaiah 65:24, *"Before they call I will answer; while they are still speaking I will hear."*
  - ✓ There is no reason to think there won't be cars, planes, computers, roads, buildings, gardens, and places to decorate and make beautiful.
  - ✓ Worship will be awesome and focus on Jesus in Jerusalem. Technology could make that possible across the planet. That worship will include resurrected humans and mortal humans.
  - ✓ All will call on Jesus' name together meaning there's probably one language again. Hooray!
  - ✓ King Jesus will reign over us in our new bodies, also. Our bodies were designed by God for life on this earth. Not to live in heaven, but to live on this earth. Isn't that interesting?

- Resurrected saints will serve in the role of priests of God. Perhaps we will be the ones teaching the mortal humans all about God and how to live dependently on Him. We will also be reigning with Him, whatever that requires. *Revelation 20:6*

- Although believers are encouraged to individually live in peace with each other and with unbelievers, we humans can never bring about world peace.

THE MORTAL HUMANS WILL STILL HAVE FREEDOM OF CHOICE.

- The Future Millenials who are mortal humans will still have the freedom of choice that God originally gave Adam and Eve. What does human freedom look like in an environment where the Healer will be healing and extending life way beyond our experience now?

- As mortal humans, the Future Millenials will still have the sin nature. If anyone chooses to rebel against the king, it's because of his/her own lusts. No one can blame the world with Jesus on the throne or the devil because he and his cohorts will be bound.

- At the end of the 1000 years, Satan will be released. He'll instigate a rebellion among non-believing mortals and finally be defeated. Doesn't it baffle you that anyone living under Jesus' perfect rule in an almost perfect world would rebel against Him? That's how strong the sin nature is.

LIFE FOREVER ON A NEW EARTH—FULLY RESTORED CREATION

- After that time, God's heaven comes to a newly restored earth. The scripture calls God's new dwelling place the New Jerusalem (Revelation 21-22). It will be absolutely beautiful.

- But there's a lot of living to come between now and then as we move around here, then move out to our new bodies, and move back to planet Earth with our King Jesus. Heaven on earth.

- When it comes to heaven, we probably have a lot more questions than answers at this time. But one thing we can know for sure. If we are living life today as though Jesus were our King ruling on earth, living dependently on Him each day, considering His presence and His will throughout the day (not just in the morning or evening), we will be a whole lot closer to understanding what real Kingdom living is all about.

- For us, the hope of heaven should transform our perspective on death. We also shouldn't long to escape this life. The point is not to escape from earth and find oneself at last in heaven, but to let God's 'heavenly' life change our earthly reality.

Let Jesus satisfy your heart with His perspective on life in the present and in the future. Then, live securely in Him during this time of waiting.

Small Group Discussion Guide

The following guide is designed for groups that meet for about 1½ hours or less. You will notice that some questions are skipped for the sake of time. These are only suggestions for you.

Ask the group to listen to the first podcast "The Need for Perspective" before coming to the first meeting. Help them find it by sending them a link to melanienewton.com/podcasts. Look for Series 13.

Gratitude: Because of Paul's emphasis on thankfulness, consider starting each lesson with everyone sharing something for which to be thankful that day.

INTRODUCTION TO STUDY

It isn't necessary to have a separate week for introducing the study. However, it is a good use of time to get to know one another and give them a vision for the study as a whole.

- Start with prayer. Pray for the group to learn from Jesus what He wants them to know and to learn to love one another well to build our community.

- Make sure everyone has a book, a schedule, and Bible / Bible app and knows how to use it. Ask if anyone is new to the Bible and plan to come alongside her during the week.

- Get acquainted with each other. Ask a general question or two such as, "Share your name, where you live, and an activity you enjoy when you have time to do so."

Introduce the study

- Look at the "Contents" page to see the lesson titles.

- Introduction Page 1. Read the top paragraph and "The Basic Study" section.

- Tell them how to find the podcasts (melanienewton.com/podcasts or any podcast platform—search "Satisfied" by Melanie Newton, Season 13). Or you can read the blogs associated with the podcasts at melanienewton.com/blog. Choose 1 & 2 Thessalonians category then scroll to find the title you want.

- Page 2: Read "New Testament Summary."

- Read "Discussion Group Guidelines." Add anything else pertinent to your group.

- Look at Lesson 2 how it is arranged. Day One is observation of the text. Make sure to do this.

The Need for Perspective Podcast

- Ask: Did anything grab your attention from the introductory podcast?

- Read through the listener guide on pages 9-10. After each of the first three paragraphs on page 10, ask, "Why do we need that?"

- Read together the italicized paragraph in the middle of page 10.

- Tell them to work on Lesson One for the next meeting.

Prayer

- Share prayer requests and pray for one another.

Recommendation: Listen to a worship song. Suggestion: "Be Exalted O God."

LESSON 1: OVERVIEW OF 1 AND 2 THESSALONIANS

Choose ahead of time which verses from the questions the group will read aloud as you proceed through the discussion. My recommendations are below.

Start with prayer.

Gratitude: Share one thing for which you are thankful today.

Day One

- Q1. Find images online of ruins at Thessalonica to show.

- Q2. Read Acts 15:1-4, answer question. Then read vv. 5-10, 13 and answer question. Discuss question at top of page 13.

- Read "Scriptural Insight." You will see those leading women in heaven one day.

- Review what perspective means and what it means to sharpen your focus on the things that matter and let go of the things that don't matter or that distract you away from what does matter.

- Read third paragraph on page 14.

- Q3. Ask everyone to share one area where they need perspective and ask the group members to write what is shared on page 20. Pray for these now and throughout the study.

Day Two

- Qs 4-7.

Day Three

- Q8.

- Q9.

- Q10. Read each set of verses and ask what made Paul thankful.

- Q11 if time, especially if you did not start with "Gratitude" sharing.

Other

- Discuss the podcast. Read "God is…" statements under "Knowing who God is." Read the first paragraph under "Knowing what He says" (page 19). Read the two aspects of trusting God. Ask, "Have you seen that in your life?" Read the first paragraph under "Knowing and Trusting God Lead to Thankfulness." Read Malachi 3:16. Read the next two paragraphs.

- Read together the italicized paragraph at the bottom of page 19.

- Pray

> *Recommendation: Listen to a worship song such as "He Lives."*

LESSON 2: PERSPECTIVE ON THE GOSPEL

Choose ahead of time which verses from the questions the group will read aloud as you proceed through the discussion. My recommendations are below.

Start with prayer.

Gratitude: Share one thing for which you are thankful today.

Day One

- Qs1-3.
- Q4. Ask each one what was their chosen verse of the week.

Day Two

- Read 1 Thessalonians 1:1-8. Q5.
- Read Romans 5:1-2. Q6.
- Qs7-9. The word for model or example referred to an indelible impression left on someone.
- Read "From the Greek."
- Q10. Read "Think About It."
- Q11. Challenge them to invest in a small group of believers in the next few months.

Day Three

- Read 1 Thessalonians 1:8-10.
- Q12. Read "Focus on the Meaning." Q13.
- Q14.
- Q15. Read Mark 13:26-27; Luke 21:27-28; and Acts 1:11. All denominations of Christians believe that Jesus is returning to earth in the future.
- Q16. Read through "What is God's wrath?"
- Q17. Read John 3:36 and 2 Thessalonians 1:7-10. Read paragraph that follows the question.
- Q18.

Other

- Discuss the podcast.
- Read together the italicized paragraph at the bottom.
- Pray

Recommendation: Listen to a worship song, such as "Even So Come, Lord Jesus Come."

LESSON 3: PERSPECTIVE ON BEING A SERVANT-LEADER

Choose ahead of time which verses from the questions the group will read aloud as you proceed through the discussion. My recommendations are below.

Start with prayer.

Gratitude: Share one thing for which you are thankful today.

Day One

- Qs1-4.

- Q5. Ask each one what was their chosen verse of the week.

Day Two

- Read Mark 10:42-45. Q6.

- Read 1 Thessalonians 2:1-6. Qs7-8 (don't read the verses).

- Read the paragraph after Q8. Q9. Read 2 Corinthians 4:2 and "Focus on the Meaning."

- Q10. Read 1 Corinthians 2:4-5.

- Q11. Read 2 Corinthians 5:9 and Galatians 1:10. Skip quote; read paragraph after it.

- Qs12-13. Q13 is good for a smaller group breakout. Give them 5-7 minutes.

Day Three

- Read John 13:13-17. Q14.

- Read 1 Thessalonians 2:7-12. Q15 and "Historical Insight."

- Skip Qs16 and 20 unless you have lots of time.

- Q17 and "Scriptural Insight."

- Qs18-19.

- Q21 first bullet.

Other

- Discuss the podcast. Read second bullet under Choice #3…"The difference between sacrifice and suffering."

- Read together the italicized paragraph at the bottom.

- Pray

> *Recommendation: Listen to a worship song, such as "Be Unto Your Name."*

LESSON 4: PERSPECTIVE ON SUFFERING

Choose ahead of time which verses from the questions the group will read aloud as you proceed through the discussion. My recommendations are below.

Start with prayer.

Gratitude: Share one thing for which you are thankful today.

Day One

- Qs1-4.
- Q5. Ask each one what was their chosen verse of the week.

Day Two

- Read 1 Thessalonians 2:13-16. Qs6-9.
- Q10. Read all the verses.
- Q11 and "Think About It." Skip next paragraph.
- Q12 and "Scriptural Insight."
- Q13. These would be good for breakout discussions.

Day Three

- Read 1 Thessalonians 2:17-20. Qs14-15. Just read Acts 17:6-9.
- Read "Scriptural Insight." Q16.
- Qs17&18. Read John 8:37-44 in Q17.
- Qs18-20. Read "From the Greek" and "Scriptural Insight."
- Qs21-22.

Other

- Discuss the podcast, especially the "look-imagine-see dragon" part.
- Read together the italicized paragraph at the bottom.
- Pray

Recommendation: Listen to a worship song, such as "Whom Shall I Fear?"

LESSON 5: PERSPECTIVE ON FAITHFUL ENDURANCE

Choose ahead of time which verses from the questions the group will read aloud as you proceed through the discussion. My recommendations are below.

Start with prayer.

Gratitude: Share one thing you have had to endure and what you learned from that.

Read Deuteronomy 8:2. God uses our suffering for our good.

Day One

- Qs1-4.
- Q5. Ask each one what was their chosen verse of the week.

Day Two

- Read 1 Thessalonians 3:1-8. Q6.
- Q8. Read all the verses.
- Q9. Read all the verses and "Dependent Living."
- Qs10&11. Read all the verses.
- Q12 and "Dependent Living."
- Q13. Read all the verses and "Scriptural Insight."
- Q15 and "Think About It."
- Q16. Read the verses.

Day Three

- Read 1 Thessalonians 3:9-13.
- Qs17-19 and "Think About It."
- Qs20&21.
- Q21.
- Qs23&24.
- Q25. Read the verses and the paragraph that follows.
- Qs26&27.
- Q28. Read Psalm 40:1-3.

Other

- Discuss the podcast.
- Read together the italicized paragraph at the bottom.
- Pray

Recommendation: Listen to a worship song, such as "Even So, Come, Lord Jesus Come."

LESSON 6: PERSPECTIVE ON SEX AND LOVE

Choose ahead of time which verses from the questions the group will read aloud as you proceed through the discussion. My recommendations are below.

Start with prayer.

Gratitude: Share thankfulness for the ones God put in your life to demonstrate His love to you.

Day One

- Qs1-4.
- Q5. Ask each one what was their chosen verse of the week.

Day Two

- Read 1 Thessalonians 4:1-8. Q6 (don't read verses) and "Think About It."
- Read paragraph and "Historical Insight."
- Q7 and paragraph that follows it.
- Qs8&9 and "Focus on the Meaning."
- Skip Q10 unless you have time; read "Scriptural Insight."
- Q11 and "Focus on the Meaning."
- Q12, paragraph that follows, and "Scriptural Insight."
- Q13.

Day Three

- Read 1 Thessalonians 4:9-12 and "From the Greek."
- Qs16-18. Read the John and 1 John verses (Q16).
- Q19. Read 1 Timothy 2:1-4.
- Q20. Read 2 Thessalonians 3:11.
- Q21. Read the verses and the "Historical Insight."
- Qs22-24. If short of time, skip Q24. We will cover work again in Lesson 11.

Other

- Discuss the podcast, especially second bullet point on top of page 75.
- Read together the italicized paragraph at the bottom.
- Pray

> *Recommendation: Listen to a worship song, such as "Build My Life."*

LESSON 7: PERSPECTIVE ON DEATH AND BEYOND

Choose ahead of time which verses from the questions the group will read aloud as you proceed through the discussion. My recommendations are below.

Start with prayer.

Gratitude: Share one thing for which you are thankful today.

Day One

- Read 2 paragraphs before the verses. Qs1-4.
- Q5. Ask each one what was their chosen verse of the week.

Day Two

- Read 1 Thessalonians 4:13-18 and "Focus on the Meaning." Q6.
- Read 2 paragraphs and do Q7. Read John 11:11-15.
- Qs8&9. Read the verses, the "Focus on the Meaning," and the "Historical Insight."
- Q10. Read the verses and the "Scriptural Insight."
- Qs11&12 and "Scriptural Insight."
- Q13 and "Scriptural Insight."
- Qs14&15. Read "Think About It" if time.

Day Three

- Q16. Read the verses, the "Focus on the Meaning," and the paragraph that follows.
- Q17. Read and discuss Luke 24:13-16; 25-27; 30-31; and 36-43.
- Q18. Read the verses.
- Read paragraph then Qs20&21. Share creative responses.

Other

- Discuss the podcast, especially the 6 √'s at the top of page 87.
- Read together the italicized paragraph at the bottom.
- Pray

Recommendation: Listen to a worship song, such as "Even So, Come, Lord Jesus Come"

LESSON 8: PERSPECTIVE ON LIVING IN THE LIGHT

Choose ahead of time which verses from the questions the group will read aloud as you proceed through the discussion. My recommendations are below.

Start with prayer.

Gratitude: Share one thing you complained about recently. Give thanks instead.

Day One

- Review "puzzle pieces" paragraph. Qs1-2. Skip Qs3&4 to save time for the rest of the lesson.
- Q5. Ask each one what was their chosen verse of the week.

Day Two

- Read 1 Thessalonians 5:4-11.
- Read "Scriptural Insight," 2 paragraphs, and "Focus on the Meaning."
- Q6. Read verses.
- Q7. Skip Mark verses.
- Qs8&9. Read Ephesians verses and "Focus on the Meaning." Skip "Scriptural Insight."
- Q10, paragraph that follows, and "Scriptural Insight."
- Q11. Skip "Focus on the Meaning."
- Qs12&13.

Day Three

- Read 1 Thessalonians 5:12-15. Q14. Read 1 Timothy verses and "Scriptural Insight."
- Qs16&17.
- Read 1 Thessalonians 5:16-22, paragraph, then Qs18&19.
- Read "Dependent Living."
- Qs20&21 and "Dependent Living."
- Q22 and "Focus on the Meaning."
- Q23.
- Q25.

Other

- Discuss the podcast. Review by reading through the √'s on page 100.
- Read together the italicized paragraph at the bottom.
- Pray

Recommendation: Listen to a worship song, such as "Even So, Come, Lord Jesus Come."

LESSON 9: PERSPECTIVE ON GOD'S JUSTICE

Choose ahead of time which verses from the questions the group will read aloud as you proceed through the discussion. My recommendations are below.

Start with prayer.

Gratitude: Share one thing for which you are thankful today.

Day One

- Read "Historical Insight" and "puzzle pieces" paragraph. Qs1-4.
- Q5. Ask each one what was their chosen verse of the week.

Day Two

- Read 2 Thessalonians 1:5-10 and "Focus on the Meaning."
- Q6. Read Romans 3:21-16 and "Think About It."
- Qs7&8. Read "Scriptural Insight" and "Focus on the Meaning."
- Q9 (read Matthew verses) and Q10 (don't read verses). Read "Think About It."
- Read paragraph then do Q11, "Focus on the Meaning," and paragraph that follows.
- Q13 and "Think About It."
- Qs14&15.

Day Three

- Read 2 Thessalonians 1:1-4, 11-12. Q16 and "Think About It."
- Q17 and "Focus on the Meaning."
- Q18.
- Q19. Read verses and "Scriptural Insight."
- Q20.

Other

- Discuss the podcast.
- Read together the italicized paragraph at the bottom.
- Pray

Recommendation: Listen to a worship song, such as "Before the Throne of God Above."

LESSON 10: PERSPECTIVE ON THE GREAT TRIBULATION

Choose ahead of time which verses from the questions the group will read aloud as you proceed through the discussion. My recommendations are below.

Start with prayer.

Gratitude: Share one thing for which you are thankful today.

Day One

- Review "puzzle pieces" paragraph. Qs1-4.
- Q5. Ask each one what was their chosen verse of the week.

Day Two

- Read 1 Thessalonians 2:1-12. Skip "Scriptural Insight."
- Q6 and "Scriptural Insight" after it. Read paragraph about the three signs.
- Restrainer: Q7 and "Think About It" and "Scriptural Insight."
- Rebellion: Read "From the Greek," two paragraphs, and Q8 (all verses).
- Man of lawlessness: Paragraph, Q9, and "Think About It."
- Q10. Read Daniel verses. Q12 and "From the Greek."
- Q13, "Focus on the Meaning," and paragraph that follows.
- Q15. Do Q16 if time.

Day Three

- Read 2 Thessalonians 2:13-17. Q17 and "Focus on the Meaning."
- Qs18&19. Read the verses and "Focus on the Meaning."
- Q20 and "Focus on the Meaning."
- Qs21&22.

Other

- Discuss the podcast, especially "What we can know for sure" points on second page.
- Read together the italicized paragraph at the bottom.
- Pray

Recommendation: Listen to a worship song, such as "Even So, Come, Lord Jesus Come."

LESSON 11: PERSPECTIVE ON LIFE IN THE WAITING

Choose ahead of time which verses from the questions the group will read aloud as you proceed through the discussion. My recommendations are below.

Start with prayer.

Gratitude: Share thankfulness for work you do and jobs you have had.

Day One

- Qs1-4. Skip Q4 to save time.
- Q5. Ask each one what was their chosen verse of the week.

Day Two

- Read 2 Thessalonians 3:1-5. Qs6&7 and "Focus on the Meaning."
- Q8. Read Colossians verses.
- Q9. Don't read Acts verses.
- Q10. Only read the Romans verses. Read "Scriptural Insight."
- Q11. Select verses to read. Read "Scriptural Insight."
- Qs12&13.

Day Three

- Read 2 Thessalonians 3:6-15. Read "From the Greek."
- Q15 and "Scriptural Insight."
- Q16 and "Focus on the Meaning."
- Q17 and "From the Greek."
- Q18. Skip "Scriptural Insight."
- Q19. Skip "Think About It."
- Q20. Read the Colossians and Ephesians verses.
- Q21. Read verses.
- Read 2 Thessalonians 3:16-18. Q23 and paragraph that follows it.
- Qs24-26. Read "Historical Insight."

Other

- Discuss the podcast, anything that is relevant to your group.
- Read together the italicized paragraph at the bottom.
- Pray

Recommendation: Listen to a worship song, such as "Build Me Life."

EXTRA LESSON: THE REST OF THE STORY

Choose ahead of time which verses from the questions the group will read aloud as you proceed through the discussion. My recommendations are below.

Start with prayer.

Gratitude: Share one thing for which you are thankful today.

Day One

- Skip the first paragraph to save time. Read the "Scriptural Insight."
- Q1. Read the verses and "From the Greek."
- Q2. Read the verses plus the "Scriptural Insight," and answer the three questions.
- Q3 (read the Romans verses). Read "Focus on the Meaning."
- Q4.

Day Two

- Read the Deuteronomy verse and look at the timeline as a "best guess."
- Read the three paragraphs.
- Q5. Read the Revelation verses.
- Q6. Read the verses and answer the question for each set. Read "Scriptural Insight."
- Q7. Talk through this. Read the Genesis verses if you have time.
- Q8. Read the verses and answer the question for each set. Read "Scriptural Insight."
- Q9. Read the verses and discuss each. Read "Think About It."
- Q10. Read verses and "Focus on the Meaning." Read paragraph that follows.
- Q11.

Day Three

- Read paragraph and do Q12. Read the paragraph that follows and "Scriptural Insight."
- Q13. Read "Scriptural Insight."
- Q14. Read verses if you have time.
- Q15. Let anyone share their creativity or just their praise for our future.

Other

- Discuss the podcast. Read the last bullet point on the bottom of the second page (146).
- Read together the italicized paragraph at the bottom.
- Pray

Recommendation: Listen to a worship song, such as "When We All Get to Heaven."

Sources

1. Donald Grey Barnhouse, *Romans Book VI*

2. *Dr. Tom Constable's Notes on 1 Thessalonians 2020 Edition*

3. *Dr. Tom Constable's Notes on 2 Thessalonians 2020 Edition*

4. *Dr. Tom Constable's Notes on 2 Corinthians 2020 Edition*

5. Heather Zempel, *Community Is Messy*

6. John F. Walvoord, *The Rapture Question*

7. Ron Newton, *Lessons from Crunch Time Business in the Bible*

8. *The Bible Knowledge Commentary New Testament*, Walvoord and Zuck

9. *The NIV Study Bible,* Zondervan

10. Vickie Kraft, *Influential Woman*

11. *Vines Expository Dictionary of Old and New Testament Words*

12. Warren W. Wiersbe, *Be Ready*

www.ingramcontent.com/pod-product-compliance
Lightning Source LLC
Chambersburg PA
CBHW080751120626
46557CB00005B/1224